Presented To:

_____

From:

_____

Date:

_____

# 100
# Prayers of
# encouragement

Freeman-Smith, a division of Worthy Media, Inc.

134 Franklin Road, Suite 200, Brentwood, Tennessee 37027

*The quoted ideas expressed in this book (but not Scripture verses) are not, in all cases, exact quotations, as some have been edited for clarity and brevity. In all cases, the author has attempted to maintain the speaker's original intent. In some cases, quoted material for this book was obtained from secondary sources, primarily print media. While every effort was made to ensure the accuracy of these sources, the accuracy cannot be guaranteed. For additions, deletions, corrections, or clarifications in future editions of this text, please write Freeman-Smith.*

Scripture quotations are taken from:

The Holy Bible, King James Version (KJV)

The Holy Bible, New International Version (NIV) Copyright © 1973, 1978, 1984, by International Bible Society. Used by permission of Zondervan Publishing House. All rights reserved.

The Holy Bible, New King James Version (NKJV) Copyright © 1982 by Thomas Nelson, Inc. Used by permission.

Holy Bible, New Living Translation, (NLT) copyright © 1996. Used by permission of Tyndale House Publishers, Inc., Wheaton, Illinois 60189. All rights reserved.

The Message (MSG)- This edition issued by contractual arrangement with NavPress, a division of The Navigators, U.S.A. Originally published by NavPress in English as THE MESSAGE: The Bible in Contemporary Language copyright 2002-2003 by Eugene Peterson. All rights reserved.

New Century Version®. (NCV) Copyright © 1987, 1988, 1991 by Word Publishing, a division of Thomas Nelson, Inc. All rights reserved. Used by permission.

The New American Standard Bible®, (NASB) Copyright © 1960, 1962, 1963, 1968, 1971, 1972, 1973, 1975, 1977, 1995 by The Lockman Foundation. Used by permission.

The Holman Christian Standard Bible™ (HCSB) Copyright © 1999, 2000, 2001 by Holman Bible Publishers. Used by permission.

Cover Design by Kim Russell / Wahoo Designs
Page Layout by Bart Dawson

ISBN 978-1-60587-352-7

Printed in the United States of America

# 100
## Prayers of
## encouragement

# Introduction

Today and every day, the sun rises upon a world filled with God's presence and His love. As believing Christians, we have so many reasons to be hopeful: The Father is in His heaven, His love is everlasting, and we, His children, are blessed beyond measure. Yet sometimes we find ourselves distracted by the demands, the frustrations, and the uncertainties of daily life. But even during our darkest days, God never leaves us for an instant. And even when our hopes are dimmed, God's light still shines brightly. As followers of God's Son, we are called to search for that light—and to keep searching for it as long as we live.

This text celebrates the hope that springs from the promises contained in God's Holy Word. The ideas on these pages are intended to encourage you, and they're intended to help you encourage others. Each chapter contains a Bible verse, thought-provoking quotations, a brief essay, and a prayer—all of which can lift your spirits and guide your path.

So today, as you embark upon the next step of your life's journey, think of ways that you can find—and share—the promises that God has made to those who choose to follow in the footsteps of His Son. When you do, you'll discover that encouragement is like honey: It's hard to spread it around without getting some on yourself.

# The Power of Encouragement

*Do not let any unwholesome talk come out of your mouths, but only what is helpful for building others up according to their needs, that it may benefit those who listen.*

*Ephesians 4:29 NIV*

Life is a team sport, and all of us need occasional pats on the back from our teammates. As Christians, we are called upon to spread the Good News of Christ, and we are also called to spread a message of encouragement and hope to the world.

Whether you realize it or not, many people with whom you come in contact every day are in desperate need of a smile or an encouraging word. The world can be a difficult place, and countless friends and family members may be troubled by the challenges of everyday life. Since you don't always know who needs your help, the best strategy is to try to encourage all the people who cross your path. So today, be a world-class source of encouragement to everyone you meet. Never has the need been greater.

We do have the ability to encourage or discourage each other with the words we say. In order to maintain a positive mood, our hearts must be in good condition.

*Annie Chapman*

The truest help we can render an afflicted man is not to take his burden from him, but to call out his best energy, that he may be able to bear the burden himself.

*Phillips Brooks*

So often we think that to be encouragers we have to produce great words of wisdom when, in fact, a few simple syllables of sympathy and an arm around the shoulder can often provide much needed comfort.

*Florence Littauer*

## Today's Prayer

*Dear Heavenly Father, because I am Your child, I am blessed. You have loved me eternally, cared for me faithfully, and saved me through the gift of Your Son Jesus. Just as You have lifted me up, Lord, let me lift up others in a spirit of encouragement and optimism and hope. And, if I can help a fellow traveler, even in a small way, Dear Lord, may the glory be Yours. Amen*

# Put God in His Rightful Place

*Do not have other gods besides Me.*

*Exodus 20:3 HCSB*

As you think about the nature of your relationship with God, remember this: you will always have some type of relationship with Him—it is inevitable that your life must be lived in relationship to God. The question is not if you will have a relationship with Him; the burning question is whether that relationship will be one that seeks to honor Him.

Are you willing to place God first in your life? And, are you willing to welcome Him into your heart? Unless you can honestly answer these questions with a resounding yes, then your relationship with God isn't what it could be or should be. Thankfully, God is always available, He's always ready to forgive, and He's waiting to hear from you now. The rest, of course, is up to you.

When all else is gone, God is still left. Nothing changes Him.

*Hannah Whitall Smith*

If God has the power to create and sustain the universe, He is more than able to sustain your marriage and your ministry, your faith and your finances, your hope and your health.

*Anne Graham Lotz*

Love has its source in God, for love is the very essence of His being.

*Kay Arthur*

It is when we come to the Lord in our nothingness, our powerlessness and our helplessness that He then enables us to love in a way which, without Him, would be absolutely impossible.

*Elisabeth Elliot*

## Today's Prayer

*Dear Lord, Your love is eternal and Your laws are everlasting. When I obey Your commandments, I am blessed. Today, I invite You to reign over every corner of my heart. I will have faith in You, Father. I will sense Your presence; I will accept Your love; I will trust Your will; and I will praise You for the Savior of my life: Your Son Jesus. Amen*

# Christ's Abundance

*I have come that they may have life, and that they may have it more abundantly.*

John 10:10 NKJV

The familiar words of John 10:10 convey this promise: Jesus came to this earth so that you might have a life of abundance. But what, precisely, did Christ mean when He talked of the abundant life? Was He promising His followers an abundance of fame and fortune? Hardly. The Prince of Peace came to this world, not to give it prosperity, but to give it salvation. Thankfully for Christians, our Savior's abundance is both spiritual and eternal; it never falters—even if we do—and it never dies. We need only to open our hearts to Him, and His grace becomes ours.

The spiritual abundance that Jesus promises is, indeed, available to you. Your task, as a follower of the One from Galilee, is to accept Christ's abundance and to claim His gifts. The fullness of life in Christ can—and should—be yours, but no one can claim those riches on your behalf . . . you must claim them for yourself.

Do you sincerely seek the riches that our Savior offers to those who give themselves to Him? Then follow Him completely and obey Him without reservation. Follow Him today, tomorrow, and every day that you live.

When you do, you will receive the love and the abundance that He has promised.

Seek first the personal transformation that is available through a genuine relationship with Christ, and then claim the joy, the peace, and the spiritual abundance that the Shepherd offers His sheep.

---

The gift of God is eternal life, spiritual life, abundant life through faith in Jesus Christ, the Living Word of God.

*Anne Graham Lotz*

The only way you can experience abundant life is to surrender your plans to Him.

*Charles Stanley*

The man who lives without Jesus is the poorest of the poor, whereas no one is so rich as the man who lives in His grace.

*Thomas à Kempis*

## Today's Prayer

*Dear Lord, You have offered me the gift of abundance through Your Son. Thank You, Father, for the abundant life that is mine through Christ Jesus. Let me accept His gifts and use them always to glorify You. Amen*

# Hope Is Contagious

*Patience and encouragement come from God. And I pray that God will help you all agree with each other the way Christ Jesus wants.*

*Romans 15:5 NCV*

Are you a hopeful, optimistic, encouraging believer? And do you associate with like-minded people? Hopefully so.

Hope, like other human emotions, is contagious. When we associate with hope-filled Christians, we are encouraged by their faith and optimism. But, if we spend too much time in the company of naysayers and pessimists, our attitudes, like theirs, tend to be cynical and negative.

As a faithful follower of the One from Galilee, you have every reason to be hopeful, and you have every reason to share your hopes with others. So today, look for reasons to celebrate God's endless blessings. And while you're at it, look for people who will join you in the celebration. You'll be better for their company, and they'll be better for yours.

Always stay connected to people and seek out things that bring you joy. Dream with abandon. Pray confidently.

*Barbara Johnson*

If I am asked how we are to get rid of discouragements, I can only say, as I have had to say of so many other wrong spiritual habits, we must give them up. It is never worth while to argue against discouragement. There is only one argument that can meet it, and that is the argument of God.

*Hannah Whitall Smith*

The glory of friendship is not the outstretched hand, or the kindly smile, or the joy of companionship. It is the spiritual inspiration that comes to one when he discovers that someone else believes in him and is willing to trust him with his friendship.

*Corrie ten Boom*

## Today's Prayer

*Dear Lord, let me celebrate the accomplishments of others. Make me a source of genuine, lasting encouragement to my family and friends. And let my words and deeds be worthy of Your Son, the One who gives me strength and salvation, this day and for all eternity. Amen*

# Today Is a New Beginning

*You are being renewed in the spirit of your minds; you put on the new man, the one created according to God's likeness in righteousness and purity of the truth.*

*Ephesians 4:23-24 HCSB*

Each new day offers countless opportunities to serve God, to seek His will, and to obey His teachings. But each day also offers countless opportunities to stray from God's commandments and to wander far from His path.

Sometimes, we wander aimlessly in a wilderness of our own making, but God has better plans for us. And, whenever we ask Him to renew our strength and guide our steps, He does so.

Consider this day a new beginning. Consider it a fresh start, a renewed opportunity to serve your Creator with willing hands and a loving heart. Ask God to renew your sense of purpose as He guides your steps. Today is a glorious opportunity to serve God. Seize that opportunity while you can; tomorrow may indeed be too late.

No matter how badly we have failed, we can always get up and begin again. Our God is the God of new beginnings.

*Warren Wiersbe*

No man need stay the way he is.

*Harry Emerson Fosdick*

More often than not, when something looks like it's the absolute end, it is really the beginning.

*Charles Swindoll*

When you're through changing, you're through!

*John Maxwell*

## Today's Prayer

*O Lord, my Creator, conform me to Your image. Create in me a clean heart, a new heart that reflects Your love for me. When I need to change, change me, Lord, and make me new. Amen*

# The Greatest of These

*But now abide faith, hope, love, these three; but the greatest of these is love.*

*1 Corinthians 13:13 NASB*

We are commanded (not advised, not encouraged…commanded!) to love one another just as Christ loved us (see John 13:34). The beautiful words of 1st Corinthians 13 remind us that love is God's commandment: Faith is important, of course. So, too, is hope. But, love is more important still. That's a tall order, but as Christians, we are obligated to follow it.

Christ showed His love for us on the cross, and we are called upon to return Christ's love by sharing it. Today, let us spread Christ's love to families, friends, and even strangers, so that through us, others might come to know Him.

Love always means sacrifice.

*Elisabeth Elliot*

Love is an attribute of God. To love others is evidence of a genuine faith.

*Kay Arthur*

You can be sure you are abiding in Christ if you are able to have a Christlike love toward the people that irritate you the most.

*Vonette Bright*

Suppose that I understand the Bible. And, suppose that I am the greatest preacher who ever lived! The Apostle Paul wrote that unless I have love, "I am nothing."

*Billy Graham*

Christian love, either towards God or towards man, is an affair of the will.

*C. S. Lewis*

## Today's Prayer

*Lord, love is Your commandment. Help me always to remember that the gift of love is a precious gift indeed. Let me nurture love and treasure it, today and forever. Amen*

# God Can Handle It

*I will lift up my eyes to the hills. From whence comes my help? My help comes from the Lord, Who made heaven and earth.*

*Psalm 121:1-2 NKJV*

It's a promise that is made over and over again in the Bible: Whatever "it" is, God can handle it.

Life isn't always easy. Far from it! Sometimes, life can be very, very difficult, indeed. But even when the storm clouds form overhead, even during our most stressful moments, we're protected by a loving Heavenly Father.

When we're worried, God can reassure us; when we're sad, God can comfort us. When our hearts are broken, God is not just near; He is here. So we must lift our thoughts and prayers to Him. When we do, He will answer our prayers. Why? Because He is our Shepherd, and He has promised to protect us now and forever.

God is God whether we recognize it or not. Nothing about that can change, except us.

*Lisa Whelchel*

Either we are adrift in chaos or we are individuals, created, loved, upheld and placed purposefully, exactly where we are. Can you believe that? Can you trust God for that?

*Elisabeth Elliot*

God is in control, and therefore in everything I can give thanks, not because of the situation, but because of the One who directs and rules over it.

*Kay Arthur*

The choice for me is to either look at all things I have lost or the things I have. To live in fear or to live in hope. Hope comes from knowing I have a sovereign, loving God who is in every event in my life.

*Lisa Beamer*

## Today's Prayer

*Heavenly Father, You never leave or forsake me. You are always with me, protecting me and encouraging me. Whatever this day may bring, I thank You for Your love and Your strength. Let me lean upon You, Father, this day and forever. Amen*

# Be Enthusiastic!

*Whatever you do, work at it with all your heart, as working for the Lord, not for men.*

*Colossians 3:23 NIV*

Do you see each day as a glorious opportunity to serve God and to do His will? Are you enthused about life, or do you struggle through each day giving scarcely a thought to God's blessings? Are you constantly praising God for His gifts, and are you sharing His Good News with the world? And are you excited about the possibilities for service that God has placed before you, whether at home, at work, at church, or at school? You should be.

You are the recipient of Christ's sacrificial love. Accept it enthusiastically and share it fervently. Jesus deserves your enthusiasm; the world deserves it; and you deserve the experience of sharing it.

Don't take hold of a thing unless you want that thing to take hold of you.

*E. Stanley Jones*

We act as though comfort and luxury were the chief requirements of life, when all we need to make us really happy is something to be enthusiastic about.

*Charles Kingsley*

God is the giver, and we are the receivers. And His richest gifts are bestowed not upon those who do the greatest things, but upon those who accept His abundance and His grace.

*Hannah Whitall Smith*

When we wholeheartedly commit ourselves to God, there is nothing mediocre or run-of-the-mill about us. To live for Christ is to be passionate about our Lord and about our lives.

*Jim Gallery*

## Today's Prayer

*Dear Lord, let me be an enthusiastic participant in life. And let my enthusiasm bring honor and glory to You. Amen*

# Guard Your Thoughts

*Finally brothers, whatever is true, whatever is honorable, whatever is just, whatever is pure, whatever is lovely, whatever is commendable—if there is any moral excellence and if there is any praise—dwell on these things.*

*Philippians 4:8 HCSB*

Are you an optimistic, hopeful, enthusiastic Christian? You should be. After all, as a believer, you have every reason to be optimistic about life here on earth and life eternal. As English clergyman William Ralph Inge observed, "No Christian should be a pessimist, for Christianity is a system of radical optimism." Inge's words are most certainly true, but sometimes, you may find yourself pulled down by tough times. If you find yourself discouraged, exhausted, or both, then it's time to ask yourself these questions: what's bothering you, and why?

If you're worried by the inevitable challenges of everyday living, God wants to have a little talk with you. After all, the ultimate battle has already been won on the cross at Calvary. And if your life has been transformed by Christ's sacrifice, then you, as a recipient of God's grace, have every reason to live courageously.

Are you willing to trust God's plans for your life, in good times and turbulent times? Hopefully, you will trust

Him completely. Proverbs 3:5-6 makes it clear: "Trust in the Lord with all your heart, and lean not on your own understanding; in all your ways acknowledge Him, and He shall direct your paths" (NKJV).

So make this promise to yourself and keep it—vow to be a hope-filled Christian. Think optimistically about your life, your profession, your family, your future, and your purpose for living. Trust your hopes, not your fears. Take time to celebrate God's glorious creation. And then, when you've filled your heart with hope and gladness, share your optimism with others. They'll be better for it, and so will you.

---

Attitude is the mind's paintbrush; it can color any situation.

*Barbara Johnson*

## Today's Prayer

*Dear Lord, I will focus on Your love, Your power, Your promises, and Your Son. When I am weak, I will turn to You for strength; when I am worried, I will turn to You for comfort; when I am troubled, I will turn to You for patience and perspective. Help me guard my thoughts, Lord, so that I may honor You this day and forever. Amen*

# The Morning Watch

*Every morning he wakes me. He teaches me to listen like a student. The Lord God helps me learn...*

Isaiah 50:4-5 NCV

Each new day is a gift from God, and if you are wise, you will spend a few quiet moments each morning thanking the Giver. When you do, you'll discover that time spent with God can lift your spirits and relieve your stress.

Warren Wiersbe writes, "Surrender your mind to the Lord at the beginning of each day." And that's sound advice. When you begin each day with your head bowed and your heart lifted, you are reminded of God's love, His protection, and His commandments. Then, you can align your priorities for the coming day with the teachings and commandments that God has placed upon your heart.

So, if you've acquired the unfortunate habit of trying to "squeeze" God into the corners of your life, it's time to reshuffle the items on your to-do list by placing God first. And if you haven't already done so, form the habit of spending quality time with your Father in heaven. He deserves it . . . and so do you.

How motivating it has been for me to view my early morning devotions as time of retreat alone with Jesus, Who desires that I "come with Him by myself to a quiet place" in order to pray, read His Word, listen for His voice, and be renewed in my spirit.

*Anne Graham Lotz*

I suggest you discipline yourself to spend time daily in a systematic reading of God's Word. Make this "quiet time" a priority that nobody can change.

*Warren Wiersbe*

A person with no devotional life generally struggles with faith and obedience.

*Charles Stanley*

## Today's Prayer

*Lord, help me to hear Your direction for my life in the quiet moments when I study Your Holy Word. And as I go about my daily activities, let everything that I say and do be pleasing to You. Amen*

# Accepting Christ

*We know very well that we are not set right with God by rule-keeping but only through personal faith in Jesus Christ.*

*Galatians 2:16 MSG*

God's love for you is deeper and more profound than you can imagine. God's love for you is so great that He sent His only Son to this earth to die for your sins and to offer you the priceless gift of eternal life. Now, you must decide whether or not to accept God's gift. Will you ignore it or embrace it? Will you return it or neglect it? Will you accept Christ, or will you turn from Him?

Your decision to accept Christ is the pivotal decision of your life. It is a decision that you cannot ignore. It is a decision that is yours and yours alone. It is a decision with profound consequences, both earthly and eternal. Accept God's gift: Accept Christ today.

Surrender to the Lord is not a tremendous sacrifice, not an agonizing performance. It is the most sensible thing you can do.

*Corrie ten Boom*

Choose Jesus Christ! Deny yourself, take up the Cross, and follow Him—for the world must be shown. The world must see, in us, a discernible, visible, startling difference.

*Elisabeth Elliot*

When you and I place our faith in Jesus Christ and invite Him to come live within us, the Holy Spirit comes upon us, and the power of God overshadows us, and the life of Jesus is born within us.

*Anne Graham Lotz*

## Today's Prayer

*Dear Lord, You sent Your Son to this earth that we might have the gift of eternal life. Thank You, Father, for that priceless gift. Help me to share the wondrous message of Jesus with others so that they, too, might accept Him as their Savior. And, let me praise You always for the new life You have given me, a life that is both abundant and eternal. Amen*

# Be a Cheerful Christian

*A cheerful heart has a continual feast.*

*Proverbs 15:15 HCSB*

Christ promises us lives of abundance and joy, but He does not force His joy upon us. We must claim His joy for ourselves, and when we do, Jesus, in turn, fills our spirits with His power and His love. Few things in life are more sad, or, for that matter, more absurd, than a grumpy Christian.

How can we receive from Christ the joy that is rightfully ours? By giving Him what is rightfully His: our hearts and our souls.

When we earnestly commit ourselves to the Savior of mankind, when we place Jesus at the center of our lives and trust Him as our personal Savior, He will transform us, not just for today, but for all eternity. Then we, as God's children, can share Christ's joy and His message with a world that needs both.

We may run, walk, stumble, drive, or fly, but let us never lose sight of the reason for the journey, or miss a chance to see a rainbow on the way.

*Gloria Gaither*

When we bring sunshine into the lives of others, we're warmed by it ourselves. When we spill a little happiness, it splashes on us.

*Barbara Johnson*

Be assured, my dear friend, that it is no joy to God in seeing you with a dreary countenance.

*C. H. Spurgeon*

Christ can put a spring in your step and a thrill in your heart. Optimism and cheerfulness are products of knowing Christ.

*Billy Graham*

## Today's Prayer

*Dear Lord, You have given me so many reasons to celebrate. Today, let me choose an attitude of cheerfulness. Let me be a joyful Christian, Lord, quick to smile and slow to anger. And, let me share Your goodness with all whom I meet so that Your love might shine in me and through me. Amen*

# Confident Christianity

*You are my hope; O Lord GOD, You are my confidence.*

*Psalm 71:5 NASB*

Sometimes, even the most devout Christians can become discouraged. Discouragement, however, is not God's way; He is a God of possibility not negativity. We Christians have many reasons to be confident. God is in His heaven; Christ has risen, and we are the sheep of His flock.

Are you a confident Christian? You should be. God's grace is eternal and His promises are unambiguous. So count your blessings, not your hardships. And live courageously. God is the Giver of all things good, and He watches over you today and forever.

Bible hope is confidence in the future.

*Warren Wiersbe*

If we indulge in any confidence that is not grounded on the Rock of Ages, our confidence is worse than a dream, it will fall on us and cover us with its ruins, causing sorrow and confusion.

*C. H. Spurgeon*

Jesus gives us the ultimate rest, the confidence we need, to escape the frustration and chaos of the world around us.

*Billy Graham*

God's omniscience can instill you with a supernatural confidence that can transform your life.

*Bill Hybels*

## Today's Prayer

*Lord, when I place my confidence in the things of this earth, I will be disappointed. But, when I put my confidence in You, I am secure. In every aspect of my life, Father, let me place my hope and my trust in Your infinite wisdom and Your boundless grace. Amen*

# Day 14

## Study His Word

*You will be a good servant of Christ Jesus, nourished by the words of the faith and of the good teaching that you have followed.*

1 Timothy 4:6 HCSB

God's Word is unlike any other book. A. W. Tozer wrote, "The purpose of the Bible is to bring men to Christ, to make them holy and prepare them for heaven. In this it is unique among books, and it always fulfills its purpose."

George Mueller observed, "The vigor of our spiritual lives will be in exact proportion to the place held by the Bible in our lives and in our thoughts." As Christians, we are called upon to study God's Holy Word and then to share it with the world.

The Bible is a priceless gift, a tool for Christians to use as they share the Good News of their Savior, Christ Jesus. Too many Christians, however, keep their spiritual tool kits tightly closed and out of sight. Jonathan Edwards advised, "Be assiduous in reading the Holy Scriptures. This is the fountain whence all knowledge in divinity must be derived. Therefore let not this treasure lie by you neglected." God's Holy Word is, indeed, a priceless, one-of-a-kind treasure. Handle it with care, but, more importantly, handle it every day.

The Bible is God's Word to man.

*Kay Arthur*

Weave the unveiling fabric of God's word through your heart and mind. It will hold strong, even if the rest of life unravels.

*Gigi Graham Tchividjian*

I need the spiritual revival that comes from spending quiet time alone with Jesus in prayer and in thoughtful meditation on His Word.

*Anne Graham Lotz*

The key to my understanding of the Bible is a personal relationship to Jesus Christ.

*Oswald Chambers*

## Today's Prayer

*Dear Lord, the Bible is Your gift to me; let me use it. When I stray from Your Holy Word, Lord, I suffer. But, when I place Your Word at the very center of my life, I am blessed. Make me a faithful student of Your Word so that I might be a faithful servant in Your world, this day and every day. Amen*

# Listening to God

*The one who is from God listens to God's words. This is why you don't listen, because you are not from God.*

John 8:47 HCSB

Sometimes God speaks loudly and clearly. More often, He speaks in a quiet voice—and if you are wise, you will be listening carefully when He does. To do so, you must carve out quiet moments each day to study His Word and sense His direction.

Can you quiet yourself long enough to listen to your conscience? Are you attuned to the subtle guidance of your intuition? Are you willing to pray sincerely and then to wait quietly for God's response? Hopefully so. Usually God refrains from sending His messages on stone tablets or city billboards. More often, He communicates in subtler ways. If you sincerely desire to hear His voice, you must listen carefully, and you must do so in the silent corners of your quiet, willing heart.

When we come to Jesus stripped of pretensions, with a needy spirit, ready to listen, He meets us at the point of need.

*Catherine Marshall*

In the soul-searching of our lives, we are to stay quiet so we can hear Him say all that He wants to say to us in our hearts.

*Charles Swindoll*

The first service one owes to others in the fellowship consists in listening to them. Just as love of God begins in listening to His Word, so the beginning of love for the brethren is learning to listen to them.

*Dietrich Bonhoeffer*

The center of power is not to be found in summit meetings or in peace conferences. It is not in Peking or Washington or the United Nations, but rather where a child of God prays in the power of the Spirit for God's will to be done in her life, in her home, and in the world around her.

*Ruth Bell Graham*

## Today's Prayer

*Lord, give me the wisdom to be a good listener. Help me listen carefully to my family, to my friends, and—most importantly—to You. Amen*

# God Protects

*When you pass through the waters, I will be with you; and through the rivers, they shall not overflow you. When you walk through the fire, you shall not be burned, nor shall the flame scorch you. For I am the Lord your God, The Holy One of Israel, your Savior.*

*Isaiah 43:2-3 NKJV*

As life here on earth unfolds, all of us encounter occasional disappointments and setbacks: Those occasional visits from Old Man Trouble are simply a fact of life, and none of us are exempt. When tough times arrive, we may be forced to rearrange our plans and our priorities. But even on our darkest days, we must remember that God's love remains constant.

The fact that we encounter adversity is not nearly so important as the way we choose to deal with it. When tough times arrive, we have a clear choice: we can begin the difficult work of tackling our troubles . . . or not. When we summon the courage to look Old Man Trouble squarely in the eye, he usually blinks. But, if we refuse to address our problems, even the smallest annoyances have a way of growing into king-sized catastrophes.

As believers, we know that God loves us and that He will protect us. In times of hardship, He will comfort us; in times of sorrow, He will dry our tears. When we are troubled, or weak, or sorrowful, God is always with us. We must build our lives on the rock that cannot be shaken: we must trust in God. And then, we must get on with the hard work of tackling our problems . . . because if we don't, who will? Or should?

---

Troubles we bear trustfully can bring us a fresh vision of God and a new outlook on life, an outlook of peace and hope.

*Billy Graham*

The sermon of your life in tough times ministers to people more powerfully than the most eloquent speaker.

*Bill Bright*

## Today's Prayer

*Dear Lord, when I face the inevitable disappointments of life, give me perspective and faith. When I am discouraged, give me the strength to trust Your promises and follow Your will. Then, when I have done my best, Father, let me live with the assurance that You are firmly in control, and that Your love endures forever. Amen*

# Day 17

# Time for Renewal

*I will give you a new heart and put a new spirit within you.*

*Ezekiel 36:26 HCSB*

Even the most inspired Christians can, from time to time, find themselves running on empty. The demands of daily life can drain us of our strength and rob us of the joy that is rightfully ours in Christ. When we find ourselves tired, discouraged, or worse, there is a source from which we can draw the power needed to recharge our spiritual batteries. That source is God.

God intends that His children lead joyous lives filled with abundance and peace. But sometimes, abundance and peace seem very far away. It is then that we must turn to God for renewal, and when we do, He will restore us.

Are you tired or troubled? Turn your heart toward God in prayer. Are you weak or worried? Take the time—or, more accurately, make the time—to delve deeply into God's Holy Word. Are you spiritually depleted? Call upon fellow believers to support you, and call upon Christ to renew your spirit and your life. When you do, you'll discover that the Creator of the universe stands always ready and always able to create a new sense of wonderment and joy in you.

God is not running an antique shop! He is making all things new!

*Vance Havner*

He is the God of wholeness and restoration.

*Stormie Omartian*

In those desperate times when we feel like we don't have an ounce of strength, He will gently pick up our heads so that our eyes can behold something—something that will keep His hope alive in us.

*Kathy Troccoli*

Repentance removes old sins and wrong attitudes, and it opens the way for the Holy Spirit to restore our spiritual health.

*Shirley Dobson*

## Today's Prayer

*Lord, You are my rock and my strength. When I grow weary, let me turn my thoughts and my prayers to You. When I am discouraged, restore my faith in You. Let me always trust in Your promises, Lord, and let me draw strength from those promises and from Your unending love. Amen*

# Giving Thanks to the Creator

*In everything give thanks; for this is the will of God in Christ Jesus for you.*

*1 Thessalonians 5:18 NKJV*

Psalm 145 makes this promise: "The LORD is gracious and compassionate, slow to anger and rich in love. The LORD is good to all; he has compassion on all he has made" (vv. 8-9 NIV).

Most of us have been blessed beyond measure, but sometimes, as busy Christians living in a demanding world, we are sometimes slow to count our gifts and even slower to give thanks to the Giver. Our blessings include life and health, family and friends, freedom and possessions—for starters. And those blessings are multiplied when we share them with others.

As the old saying goes, "When we drink the water, we should remember the spring." May we, who have been so richly blessed, give thanks for our gifts—and may we demonstrate our gratitude by sharing them.

The act of thanksgiving is a demonstration of the fact that you are going to trust and believe God.

*Kay Arthur*

God is in control, and therefore in everything I can give thanks, not because of the situation, but because of the One who directs and rules over it.

*Kay Arthur*

God is worthy of our praise and is pleased when we come before Him with thanksgiving.

*Shirley Dobson*

God's kindness is not like the sunset—brilliant in its intensity, but dying every second. God's generosity keeps coming and coming and coming.

*Bill Hybels*

## Today's Prayer

*Heavenly Father, Your gifts are greater than I can imagine. May I live each day with thanksgiving in my heart and praise on my lips. Thank You for the gift of Your Son and for the promise of eternal life. Let me share the joyous news of Jesus Christ, and let my life be a testimony to His love and His grace. Amen*

# Let God Guide the Way

*The true children of God are those who let God's Spirit lead them.*

*Romans 8:14 NCV*

The Bible promises that God will guide you if you let Him. Your job, of course, is to let Him. But sometimes, you will be tempted to do otherwise. Sometimes, you'll be tempted to go along with the crowd; other times, you'll be tempted to do things your way, not God's way. When you feel those temptations, resist them.

What will you allow to guide you through the coming day: your own desires (or, for that matter, the desires of your friends)? Or will you allow God to lead the way? The answer should be obvious. You should let God be your guide. When you entrust your life to Him completely and without reservation, God will give you the strength to meet any challenge, the courage to face any trial, and the wisdom to live in His righteousness. So trust Him today and seek His guidance. When you do, your next step will be the right one.

Are you serious about wanting God's guidance to become a personal reality in your life? The first step is to tell God that you know you can't manage your own life; that you need his help.

*Catherine Marshall*

Only He can guide you to invest your life in worthwhile ways. This guidance will come as you "walk" with Him and listen to Him.

*Henry Blackaby and Claude King*

It's a bit like river rafting with an experienced guide. You may begin to panic when the guide steers you straight into a steep waterfall, especially if another course appears much safer. Yet, after you've emerged from the swirling depths and wiped the spray from your eyes, you see that just beyond the seemingly "safe" route was a series of jagged rocks. Your guide knew what he was doing after all.

*Shirley Dobson*

## Today's Prayer

*Lord, You have a plan for my life. Let me discover it and live it. Today, I will seek Your will, knowing that when I trust in You, Dear Father, I am eternally blessed. Amen*

# Facing Fears

*Don't be afraid, for I am with you. Do not be dismayed for I am your God. I will strengthen you. I will help you. I will uphold you with my victorious right hand.*

*Isaiah 41:10 NLT*

We live in a world that is, at times, a frightening place. We live in a world that is, at times, a discouraging place. We live in a world where life-changing losses can be so painful and so profound that it seems we will never recover. But, with God's help, and with the help of encouraging family members and friends, we can recover.

During the darker days of life, we are wise to remember the words of Jesus, who reassured His disciples, saying, "Take courage! It is I. Don't be afraid" (Matthew 14:27 NIV). Then, with God's comfort and His love in our hearts, we can offer encouragement to others. And by helping them face their fears, we can, in turn, tackle our own problems with courage, determination, and faith.

God knows that the strength that comes from wrestling with our fear will give us wings to fly.

*Paula Rinehart*

Worry is a cycle of inefficient thoughts whirling around a center of fear.

*Corrie ten Boom*

Adversity is always unexpected and unwelcomed. It is an intruder and a thief, and yet in the hands of God, adversity becomes the means through which His supernatural power is demonstrated.

*Charles Stanley*

When once we are assured that God is good, then there can be nothing left to fear.

*Hannah Whitall Smith*

## Today's Prayer

*Father, even when I walk through the valley of the shadow of death, I will fear no evil because You are with me. Thank You, Lord, for Your perfect love, a love that casts out fear and gives me strength and courage to meet the challenges of this world. Amen*

# Contagious Christianity

*Therefore, everyone who will acknowledge Me before men, I will also acknowledge him before My Father in heaven.*

Matthew 10:32 HCSB

Genuine, heartfelt Christianity can be highly contagious. When you've experienced the transforming power of God's love, you feel the need to share the Good News of His only begotten Son. So, whether you realize it or not, you can be sure that you are being led to share the story of your faith with family, with friends, and with the world.

Every believer, including you, bears responsibility for sharing God's Good News. And it is important to remember that you share your testimony through words and actions, but not necessarily in that order.

Today, don't be bashful or timid: Talk about Jesus and, while you're at it, show the world what it really means to follow Him. After all, the fields are ripe for the harvest, time is short, and the workers are surprisingly few. So please share your story today because tomorrow may indeed be too late.

To be a Christian means to forgive the inexcusable, because God has forgiven the inexcusable in you.

*C. S. Lewis*

The Holy Spirit testifies of Jesus. So when you are filled with the Holy Spirit, you speak about our Lord and really live to His honor.

*Corrie ten Boom*

Christianity, in its purest form, is nothing more than seeing Jesus. Christian service, in its purest form, is nothing more than imitating him who we see. To see his Majesty and to imitate him . . . that is the sum of Christianity.

*Max Lucado*

## Today's Prayer

*Thank You, Lord, for Your Son. His love is boundless, infinite, and eternal. Today, let me pause and reflect upon Christ's love for me, and let me share that love with all those who cross my path. And, as an expression of my love for Him, let me share Christ's saving message with a world that desperately needs His grace. Amen*

# Day 22

## Asking for Directions

*If you need wisdom—if you want to know what God wants you to do—ask him, and he will gladly tell you. He will not resent your asking.*

Genuine, heartfelt prayer produces powerful changes in us and in our world. When we lift our hearts to God, we open ourselves to a never-ending source of divine wisdom and infinite love. Jesus made it clear to His disciples: they should petition God to meet their needs. So should we.

Do you have questions about your future that you simply can't answer? Do you have needs that you simply can't meet by yourself? Do you sincerely seek to know God's unfolding plans for your life? If so, ask Him for direction, for protection, and for strength—and then keep asking Him every day that you live. Whatever your need, no matter how great or small, pray about it and have faith. God is not just near; He is here, and He's perfectly capable of answering your prayers. Now, it's up to you to ask.

Notice that we must ask. And we will sometimes struggle to hear and struggle with what we hear. But personally, it's worth it. I'm after the path of life—and he alone knows it.

*John Eldredge*

God makes prayer as easy as possible for us. He's completely approachable and available, and He'll never mock or upbraid us for bringing our needs before Him.

*Shirley Dobson*

When will we realize that we're not troubling God with our questions and concerns? His heart is open to hear us—his touch nearer than our next thought—as if no one in the world existed but us. Our very personal God wants to hear from us personally.

*Gigi Graham Tchividjian*

## Today's Prayer

*Lord, when I have questions about my purpose in life, I will turn to You. When I am weak, I will seek Your strength. When I am discouraged, Father, I will be mindful of Your love and Your grace. I will ask You for the things I need, Father, and I will trust Your answers, today and forever. Amen*

# Faith for Life

*For whatever is born of God overcomes the world. And this is the victory that has overcome the world—our faith.*

1 John 5:4 NKJV

The first element of a successful life is faith: faith in God, faith in His Son, and faith in His promises. If we place our lives in God's hands, our faith is rewarded in ways that we—as human beings with clouded vision and limited understanding—can scarcely comprehend. But, if we seek to rely solely upon our own resources, or if we seek earthly success outside the boundaries of God's commandments, we reap a bitter harvest for ourselves and for our loved ones.

Trust God today and every day that you live. Then, when you have entrusted your future to the Giver of all things good, rest assured that your future is secure, not only for today, but also for all eternity.

It is faith that saves us, not works, but the faith that saves us always produces works.

*C. H. Spurgeon*

Just as our faith strengthens our prayer life, so do our prayers deepen our faith. Let us pray often, starting today, for a deeper, more powerful faith.

*Shirley Dobson*

Faith, as Paul saw it, was a living, flaming thing leading to surrender and obedience to the commandments of Christ.

*A. W. Tozer*

Shout the shout of faith. Nothing can withstand the triumphant faith that links itself to omnipotence. For "this is the victory that overcometh the world." The secret of all successful living lies in this shout of faith.

*Hannah Whitall Smith*

## Today's Prayer

*Father, in the dark moments of my life, help me to remember that You are always near and that You can overcome any challenge. Keep me mindful of Your love and Your power, so that I may live courageously and faithfully today and every day. Amen*

# You and Your Family

*But if any widow has children or grandchildren, they should learn to practice their religion toward their own family first and to repay their parents, for this pleases God.*

1 Timothy 5:4 HCSB

As every person knows, family life is a mixture of conversations, mediations, irritations, deliberations, commiserations, frustrations, negotiations and celebrations. In other words, life in the typical family is incredibly varied.

Certainly, in the life of every family, there are moments of frustration and disappointment. Lots of them. But, for those who are lucky enough to live in the presence of a close-knit, caring clan, the rewards far outweigh the frustrations. That's why we pray fervently for our family members, and that's why we love them despite their faults.

No family is perfect, and neither is yours. But, despite the inevitable challenges and occasional hurt feelings of family life, your clan is God's gift to you. That little band of men, women, kids, and babies is a priceless treasure on temporary loan from the Father above. Give thanks to the Giver for the gift of family…and act accordingly.

A home is a place where we find direction.

*Gigi Graham Tchividjian*

One way or the other, God, who thought up the family in the first place, has the very best idea of how to bring sense to the chaos of broken relationships we see all around us. I really believe that if I remain still and listen a lot, He will share some solutions with me so I can share them with others.

*Jill Briscoe*

Living life with a consistent spiritual walk deeply influences those we love most.

*Vonette Bright*

Live in the present and make the most of your opportunities to enjoy your family and friends.

*Barbara Johnson*

## Today's Prayer

*Dear Lord, I am part of Your family, and I praise You for Your gifts and for Your love. You have also blessed me with my earthly family, and I pray for them, that they might be protected and blessed by You. Let me show love and acceptance for my family, Lord, so that through me, they might come to know and to love You. Amen*

# Worship Him Every Day

*God is Spirit, and those who worship Him must worship in spirit and truth.*

*John 4:24 HCSB*

God's Word makes it clear: we should offer our Creator the praise and worship He deserves— and we shouldn't wait until Sunday morning to do so. Yet we live in a distraction-filled society that encourages us to make praise and worship a one-day-a-week activity.

If we allow the distractions or everyday living to interfere with the practice of regular worship and praise— or if we yield to the countless temptations of our world— we find ourselves engaged in a struggle between good and evil, a clash between God and Satan. Our responses to these struggles have implications that echo throughout our families and throughout our communities.

Do you take time each day to worship your Father in heaven, or do you wait until Sunday morning to praise Him for His blessings? The answer to this question will, in large part, determine the quality and direction of your spiritual life in good times and in turbulent times.

Every day provides opportunities to put God where He belongs: at the center of our lives. When we do so, we worship Him not only with our words, but also with our deeds, and that's as it should be. For believers, God comes first. Always first.

---

When your grief presses you to the very dust, worship there.

*C. H. Spurgeon*

I am of the opinion that we should not be concerned about working for God until we have learned the meaning and delight of worshipping Him.

*A. W. Tozer*

To worship Him in truth means to worship Him honestly, without hypocrisy, standing open and transparent before Him.

*Anne Graham Lotz*

## Today's Prayer

*Heavenly Father, let today and every day be a time of worship. Let me worship You, not only with words and deeds, but also with my heart. In the quiet moments of the day, let me praise You and thank You for creating me, loving me, guiding me, and saving me. Amen*

# Constant Praise

*Through Him then, let us continually offer up a sacrifice of praise to God, that is, the fruit of lips that give thanks to His name.*

Hebrews 13:15 NASB

Sometimes, we allow ourselves to become so preoccupied with the demands of daily life that we forget to say "Thank You" to the Giver of all good gifts. But the Bible makes it clear: it pays to praise God.

Worship and praise should be a part of everything we do. Otherwise, we quickly lose perspective as we fall prey to the demands of the moment.

Do you sincerely desire to be a worthy servant of the One who has given you eternal love and eternal life? Then praise Him for who He is and for what He has done for you. Praise Him all day long, every day, for as long as you live . . . and then for all eternity.

Nothing we do is more powerful or more life-changing than praising God.

*Stormie Omartian*

Worship is an act which develops feelings for God, not a feeling for God which is expressed in an act of worship. When we obey the command to praise God in worship, our deep, essential need to be in relationship with God is nurtured.

*Eugene Peterson*

Be not afraid of saying too much in the praises of God; all the danger is of saying too little.

*Matthew Henry*

Praise God from whom all blessings flow. Praise Him all creatures here below. Praise Him above ye heavenly host. Praise Father, Son, and Holy Ghost.

*Thomas Ken*

## Today's Prayer

*Heavenly Father, I come to You today with hope in my heart and praise on my lips. I place my trust in You, Dear Lord, knowing that with You as my Protector, I have nothing to fear. I thank You, Lord, for Your grace, for Your love, and for Your Son. Amen*

# Get Involved in a Church

*And I also say to you that you are Peter, and on this rock I will build My church, and the forces of Hades will not overpower it. I will give you the keys of the kingdom of heaven, and whatever you bind on earth will have been bound in heaven, and whatever you loose on earth will have been loosed in heaven.*

*Matthew 16:18-19 HCSB*

Are you an active, contributing, member of your local fellowship? The answer to this simple question will have a profound impact on the direction of your spiritual journey and the content of your character.

If you are not currently engaged in a local church, you're missing out on an array of blessings that include, but are certainly not limited to, the life-lifting relationships that you can—and should—be experiencing with fellow believers.

So do yourself a favor: Find a congregation you're comfortable with, and join it. And once you've joined, don't just attend church out of habit. Go to church out of a sincere desire to know and worship God. When you do, you'll be blessed by the men and women who attend your fellowship, and you'll be blessed by your Creator.

You deserve to attend church, and God deserves for you to attend church, so don't delay.

---

Our churches are meant to be havens where the caste rules of the world do not apply.

*Beth Moore*

Every time a new person comes to God, every time someone's gifts find expression in the fellowship of believers, every time a family in need is surrounded by the caring church, the truth is affirmed anew: the Church triumphant is alive and well!

*Gloria Gaither*

In God's economy you will be hard-pressed to find many examples of successful "Lone Rangers."

*Luci Swindoll*

## Today's Prayer

*Dear Lord, today I pray for Your church. Let me help to feed Your flock by helping to build Your church so that others, too, might experience Your enduring love and Your eternal grace. Amen*

# Make the Most of Whatever Comes

*A man's heart plans his way, but the Lord determines his steps.*

Proverbs 16:9 HCSB

Sometimes, we must accept life on its terms, not our own. Life has a way of unfolding, not as we will, but as it will. And sometimes, there is precious little we can do to change things.

When events transpire that are beyond our control, we have a choice: we can either learn the art of acceptance, or we can make ourselves miserable as we struggle to change the unchangeable.

We must entrust the things we cannot change to God. Once we have done so, we can prayerfully and faithfully tackle the important work that He has placed before us: doing something about the things we can change . . . and doing it sooner rather than later.

Can you summon the courage and the wisdom to accept life on its own terms? If so, you'll most certainly be rewarded for your good judgment.

It is always possible to do the will of God. In every place and time it is within our power to acquiesce in the will of God.

*Elisabeth Elliot*

We must meet our disappointments, our persecutions, our malicious enemies, our provoking friends, our trials and temptations of every sort, with an attitude of surrender and trust. We must spread our wings and "mount up" to the "heavenly places in Christ" above them all, where they will lose their power to harm or distress us.

*Hannah Whitall Smith*

The one true way of dying to self is the way of patience, meekness, humility, and resignation to God.

*Andrew Murray*

## Today's Prayer

*Dear Lord, let me live in the present, not the past. Let me focus on my blessings, not my sorrows. Give me the wisdom to be thankful for the gifts that I do have, and not bitter about the things that I don't have. Let me accept what was, let me give thanks for what is, and let me have faith in what most surely will be: the promise of eternal life with You. Amen*

# Helping Others Manage Turbulent Times

*From a wise mind comes wise speech; the words of the wise are persuasive.*

*Proverbs 16:23 NLT*

If you want to help your family and friends overcome stress, then you must measure your words carefully. And that's exactly what God wants you to do. God's Word reminds us that "Reckless words pierce like a sword, but the tongue of the wise brings healing" (Proverbs 12:18 NIV).

Today, make this promise to yourself: vow to be an honest, effective, encouraging communicator at work, at home, and everyplace in between. Speak wisely, not impulsively. Use words of kindness and praise, not words of anger or derision. Learn how to be truthful without being cruel. Remember that you have the power to heal others or to injure them, to lift others up or to hold them back. And when you learn how to lift them up, you'll soon discover that you've lifted yourself up, too.

Attitude and the spirit in which we communicate are as important as the words we say.

*Charles Stanley*

Part of good communication is listening with the eyes as well as with the ears.

*Josh McDowell*

We should ask ourselves three things before we speak: Is it true? Is it kind? Does it glorify God?

*Billy Graham*

To the loved, a word of affection is a morsel, but to the love-starved, a word of affection can be a feast.

*Max Lucado*

## Today's Prayer

*Lord, You have warned me that I will be judged by the words I speak. Keep me mindful, Lord, that I have influence on many people; make me an influence for good. And, may the words that I speak today be worthy of the One who has saved me forever. Amen*

# Look for Fulfillment
# in All the Right Places

*I know what it is to be in need, and I know what it is to have plenty. I have learned the secret of being content in any and every situation, whether well fed or hungry, whether living in plenty or in want. I can do everything through him who gives me strength.*

*Philippians 4:12-13 NIV*

Everywhere we turn, or so it seems, the world promises us contentment and happiness. But the contentment that the world offers is fleeting and incomplete. Thankfully, the contentment that God offers is all encompassing and everlasting.

Happiness depends less upon our circumstances than upon our thoughts. When we turn our thoughts to God, to His gifts, and to His glorious creation, we experience the joy that God intends for His children. But, when we focus on the negative aspects of life—or when we disobey God's commandments—we cause ourselves needless suffering.

Do you sincerely want to be a contented Christian? Then set your mind and your heart upon God's love and His grace . . . and let Him take care of the rest.

Contentment is something we learn by adhering to the basics—cultivating a growing relationship with Jesus Christ, living daily, and knowing that Christ strengthens us for every challenge.

*Charles Stanley*

Father and Mother lived on the edge of poverty, and yet their contentment was not dependent upon their surroundings. Their relationship to each other and to the Lord gave them strength and happiness.

*Corrie ten Boom*

The key to contentment is to consider. Consider who you are and be satisfied with that. Consider what you have and be satisfied with that. Consider what God's doing and be satisfied with that.

*Luci Swindoll*

## Today's Prayer

*Dear Lord, You offer me contentment and peace; let me accept Your peace. Help me to trust Your Word, to follow Your commandments, and to welcome the peace of Jesus into my heart, today and forever. Amen*

# Follow Him

*Then Jesus said to His disciples, "If anyone wants to come with Me, he must deny himself, take up his cross, and follow Me. For whoever wants to save his life will lose it, but whoever loses his life because of Me will find it."*

*Matthew 16:24-25 HCSB*

Jesus walks with you. Are you walking with Him seven days a week, and not just on Sunday mornings? Are you a seven-day-a-week Christian who carries your faith with you to work each day, or do you try to keep Jesus at a "safe" distance when you're not sitting in church? Hopefully, you understand the wisdom of walking with Christ all day every day.

Jesus loved you so much that He endured unspeakable humiliation and suffering for you. How will you respond to Christ's sacrifice? Will you take up His cross and follow Him—during good times and tough times—or will you choose another path? When you place your hopes squarely at the foot of the cross, when you place Jesus squarely at the center of your life, you will be blessed.

Do you seek to fulfill God's purpose for your life? Do you seek spiritual abundance? Would you like to partake in "the peace that passes all understanding"? Then follow Christ. Follow Him by picking up His cross today and every day that you live. When you do, you will quickly discover that Christ's love has the power to change everything, including you.

---

You who suffer take heart. Christ is the answer to sorrow.

*Billy Graham*

Will you, with a glad and eager surrender, hand yourself and all that concerns you over into his hands? If you will do this, your soul will begin to know something of the joy of union with Christ.

*Hannah Whitall Smith*

In the midst of the pressure and the heat, I am confident His hand is on my life, developing my faith until I display His glory, transforming me into a vessel of honor that pleases Him!

*Anne Graham Lotz*

## Today's Prayer

*Dear Jesus, because I am Your disciple, I will trust You, I will obey Your teachings, and I will share Your Good News. You have given me life abundant and life eternal, and I will follow You today and forever. Amen*

# Live Courageously

*He will not fear bad news; his heart is confident, trusting in the Lord. His heart is assured; he will not fear.*

Psalm 112:7-8 HCSB

Every person's life is a tapestry of events: some wonderful, some not-so-wonderful, and some downright disastrous. When we visit the mountaintops of life, praising God isn't hard—in fact, it's easy. In our moments of triumph, we can bow our heads and thank God for our victories. But when we fail to reach the mountaintops, when we endure the inevitable losses that are a part of every person's life, we find it much tougher to give God the praise He deserves. Yet wherever we find ourselves, whether on the mountaintops of life or in life's darkest valleys, we must still offer thanks to God, giving thanks in all circumstances.

The next time you find yourself worried about the challenges of today or the uncertainties of tomorrow, ask yourself this question: are you really ready to place your concerns and your life in God's all-powerful, all-knowing, all-loving hands? If the answer to that question is yes—as it should be—then you can draw courage today from the source of strength that never fails: your Father in heaven.

Just as courage is faith in good, so discouragement is faith in evil, and, while courage opens the door to good, discouragement opens it to evil.

*Hannah Whitall Smith*

Seeing that a Pilot steers the ship in which we sail, who will never allow us to perish even in the midst of shipwrecks, there is no reason why our minds should be overwhelmed with fear and overcome with weariness.

*John Calvin*

The Lord is glad to open the gate to every knocking soul. It opens very freely; its hinges are not rusted, no bolts secure it. Have faith and enter at this moment through holy courage. If you knock with a heavy heart, you shall yet sing with joy of spirit. Never be discouraged!

*C. H. Spurgeon*

## Today's Prayer

*Lord, sometimes I face challenges that leave me breathless. When I am fearful, let me lean upon You. Keep me ever mindful, Lord, that You are my God, my strength, and my shield. With You by my side, I have nothing to fear. And, with Your Son Jesus as my Savior, I have received the priceless gift of eternal life. Help me to be a grateful and courageous servant this day and every day. Amen*

# Forgive Everybody

*For if you forgive people their wrongdoing, your heavenly Father will forgive you as well. But if you don't forgive people, your Father will not forgive your wrongdoing.*

*Matthew 6:14-15 HCSB*

The world holds few if any rewards for those who remain angrily focused upon the past. Still, the act of forgiveness is difficult for all but the most saintly men and women. Are you mired in the quicksand of bitterness or regret? If so, you are not only disobeying God's Word, you are also wasting your time.

Being frail, fallible, imperfect human beings, most of us are quick to anger, quick to blame, slow to forgive, and even slower to forget. Yet as Christians, we are commanded to forgive others, just as we, too, have been forgiven.

If there exists even one person—alive or dead—against whom you hold bitter feelings, it's time to forgive. Or, if you are embittered against yourself for some past mistake or shortcoming, it's finally time to forgive yourself and move on. Hatred, bitterness, and regret are not part of God's plan for your life. Forgiveness is.

The fact is, God no longer deals with us in judgment but in mercy. If people got what they deserved, this old planet would have ripped apart at the seams centuries ago. Praise God that because of His great love "we are not consumed, for his compassions never fail" (Lam. 3:22).

*Joni Eareckson Tada*

When God forgives, He forgets. He buries our sins in the sea and puts a sign on the shore saying, "No Fishing Allowed."

*Corrie ten Boom*

God expects us to forgive others as He has forgiven us; we are to follow His example by having a forgiving heart.

*Vonette Bright*

To be a Christian means to forgive the inexcusable, because God has forgiven the inexcusable in you.

*C. S. Lewis*

## Today's Prayer

*Dear Lord, let forgiveness rule my heart, even when forgiveness is difficult. Let me be Your obedient servant, Lord, and let me be a person who forgives others just as You have forgiven me. Amen*

# Defeating Negativity

*Let angry people endure the backlash of their own anger; if you try to make it better, you'll only make it worse.*

Proverbs 19:19 MSG

From experience, we know that it is easy to criticize others. And we know that it is usually far easier to find faults than to find solutions. Still, the urge to criticize others remains a powerful temptation for most of us.

Negativity is highly contagious: We give it to others who, in turn, give it back to us. This stress-inducing cycle can be broken only by positive thoughts, heartfelt prayers, encouraging words, and meaningful acts of kindness.

As thoughtful servants of a loving God, we have no valid reason—and no legitimate excuse—to be negative. So, when we are tempted to be overly critical of others, or unfairly critical of ourselves, we must use the transforming power of God's love to break the chains of negativity. We must defeat negativity before negativity defeats us.

Winners see an answer for every problem; losers see a problem in every answer.

*Barbara Johnson*

We never get anywhere—nor do our conditions and circumstances change—when we look at the dark side of life.

*Mrs. Charles E. Cowman*

To lose heart is to lose everything.

*John Eldredge*

Do not build up obstacles in your imagination. Difficulties must be studied and dealt with, but they must not be magnified by fear.

*Norman Vincent Peale*

## Today's Prayer

*Lord, let me be an expectant Christian. Let me expect the best from You, and let me look for the best in others. If I become discouraged, Father, turn my thoughts and my prayers to You. Let me trust You, Lord, to direct my life. And, let me be Your faithful, hopeful, optimistic servant every day that I live. Amen*

# During Difficult Days

*God is our refuge and strength, a very present help in trouble.*

*Psalm 46:1 NKJV*

All of us face difficult days. Sometimes even the most devout Christian men and women can become discouraged, and you are no exception. After all, you live in a world where expectations can be high and demands can be even higher.

If you find yourself enduring difficult circumstances, remember that God remains in His heaven. If you become discouraged with the direction of your day or your life, turn your thoughts and prayers to Him. He is a God of possibility, not negativity. He will guide you through your difficulties and beyond them. And then, with a renewed spirit of optimism and hope, you can thank the Giver of all things good for gifts that are simply too numerous to count.

When life is difficult, God wants us to have a faith that trusts and waits.

*Kay Arthur*

Even in the winter, even in the midst of the storm, the sun is still there. Somewhere, up above the clouds, it still shines and warms and pulls at the life buried deep inside the brown branches and frozen earth. The sun is there! Spring will come.

*Gloria Gaither*

The strengthening of faith comes from staying with it in the hour of trial. We should not shrink from tests of faith.

*Catherine Marshall*

Our heavenly Father never takes anything from his children unless he means to give them something better.

*George Mueller*

## Today's Prayer

*Dear Heavenly Father, when I am troubled, You heal me. When I am afraid, You protect me. When I am discouraged, You lift me up. During the difficult days of my life, I will trust You. And whatever my circumstances, Lord, I thank You for Your blessings, for Your love, and for Your Son. Amen*

# A Worthy Disciple

*He has showed you, O man, what is good. And what does the LORD require of you? To act justly and to love mercy and to walk humbly with your God.*

Micah 6:8 NIV

When Jesus addressed His disciples, He warned that each one must, "take up his cross and follow Me." The disciples must have known exactly what the Master meant. In Jesus' day, prisoners were forced to carry their own crosses to the location where they would be put to death. Thus, Christ's message was clear: in order to follow Him, Christ's disciples must deny themselves and, instead, trust Him completely. Nothing has changed since then.

If we are to be disciples of Christ, we must trust Him and place Him at the very center of our beings. Jesus never comes "next." He is always first.

Do you seek to be a worthy disciple of Christ? Then pick up His cross today and every day that you live. When you do, He will bless you now and forever.

Discipleship is a daily discipline: we follow Jesus a step at a time, a day at a time.

*Warren Wiersbe*

Discipleship means personal, passionate devotion to a Person, our Lord Jesus Christ.

*Oswald Chambers*

Discipleship is a decision to live by what I know about God, not by what I feel about him or myself or my neighbors.

*Eugene Peterson*

Be filled with the Holy Spirit; join a church where the members believe the Bible and know the Lord; seek the fellowship of other Christians; learn and be nourished by God's Word and His many promises. Conversion is not the end of your journey—it is only the beginning.

*Corrie ten Boom*

## Today's Prayer

*Dear Lord, thank You for the gift of Your Son Jesus, my personal Savior. Let me be a worthy disciple of Christ, and let me be ever grateful for His love. I will praise You always, Father, as I give thanks for Your Son and for Your everlasting love. Amen*

# Big Dreams

*With God's power working in us, God can do much, much more than anything we can ask or imagine.*

*Ephesians 3:20 NCV*

It takes courage to dream big dreams. You will discover that courage when you do three things: accept the past, trust God to handle the future, and make the most of the time He has given you today.

Are you excited about the opportunities of today and thrilled by the possibilities of tomorrow? Do you confidently expect God to lead you to a place of abundance, peace, and joy? And, when your days on earth are over, do you expect to receive the priceless gift of eternal life? If you trust God's promises, and if you have welcomed God's Son into your heart, then you should believe that your future is intensely and eternally bright.

No dreams are too big for God—not even yours. So start living—and dreaming—accordingly.

Allow your dreams a place in your prayers and plans. God-given dreams can help you move into the future He is preparing for you.

*Barbara Johnson*

The future lies all before us. Shall it only be a slight advance upon what we usually do? Ought it not to be a bound, a leap forward to altitudes of endeavor and success undreamed of before?

*Annie Armstrong*

Always stay connected to people and seek out things that bring you joy. Dream with abandon. Pray confidently.

*Barbara Johnson*

Set goals so big that unless God helps you, you will be a miserable failure.

*Bill Bright*

## Today's Prayer

*Dear Lord, my hope is in You. Give me the courage to face the future with certainty, and give me the wisdom to follow in the footsteps of Your Son, today and forever. Amen.*

# Put Faith Above Feelings

*Now the just shall live by faith.*

*Hebrews 10:38 NKJV*

Who is in charge of your emotions? Is it you, or have you formed the unfortunate habit of letting other people—or troubling situations—determine the quality of your thoughts and the direction of your day? If you're wise—and if you'd like to build a better life for yourself and your loved ones—you'll learn to control your emotions before your emotions control you.

Human emotions are highly variable, decidedly unpredictable, and often unreliable. Our emotions are like the weather, only far more fickle. So we must learn to live by faith, not by the ups and downs of our own emotional roller coasters.

Sometime during this day, you will probably be gripped by a strong negative feeling. Distrust it. Reign it in. Test it. And turn it over to God. Your emotions will inevitably change; God will not. So trust Him completely as you watch those negative feelings slowly evaporate into thin air—which, of course, they will.

I may no longer depend on pleasant impulses to bring me before the Lord. I must rather respond to principles I know to be right, whether I feel them to be enjoyable or not.

*Jim Elliot*

Emotions we have not poured out in the safe hands of God can turn into feelings of hopelessness and depression. God is safe.

*Beth Moore*

Don't bother much about your feelings. When they are humble, loving, brave, give thanks for them; when they are conceited, selfish, cowardly, ask to have them altered. In neither case are they you, but only a thing that happens to you. What matters is your intentions and your behavior.

*C. S. Lewis*

## Today's Prayer

*Heavenly Father, You are my strength and my refuge. As I journey through this day, I will encounter events that cause me emotional distress. Lord, when I am troubled, let me turn to You. Keep me steady, Lord, and in those difficult moments, renew a right spirit inside my heart. Amen*

# An Attitude of Gratitude

*Finally brothers, whatever is true, whatever is honorable, whatever is just, whatever is pure, whatever is lovely, whatever is commendable—if there is any moral excellence and if there is any praise—dwell on these things.*

*Philippians 4:8 HCSB*

How will you direct your thoughts today? Will you obey the words of Philippians 4:8 by dwelling upon those things that are honorable, just, and commendable? Or will you allow your thoughts to be hijacked by the negativity that seems to dominate our troubled world? Are you fearful, angry, bored, or worried? Are you so preoccupied with the concerns of this day that you fail to thank God for the promise of eternity? Are you confused, bitter, or pessimistic? If so, God wants to have a little talk with you.

God intends that you experience joy and abundance. So, today and every day hereafter, celebrate the life that God has given you by focusing your thoughts upon those things that are worthy of praise. Today, count your blessings instead of your hardships. And thank the Giver of all things good for gifts that are simply too numerous to count.

The mind is like a clock that is constantly running down. It has to be wound up daily with good thoughts.

*Fulton J. Sheen*

We shouldn't deny the pain of what happens in our lives. But, we should refuse to focus only on the valleys.

*Charles Swindoll*

Pain is inevitable, but misery is optional.

*Max Lucado*

Attitude is more important than the past, than education, than money, than circumstances, than what people do or say. It is more important than appearance, giftedness, or skill.

*Charles Swindoll*

## Today's Prayer

*Lord, I pray for an attitude that is Christlike. Whatever my circumstances, whether good or bad, triumphal or tragic, let my response reflect a God-honoring attitude of optimism, faith, and love for You. Amen*

# Accepting Advice

*A wise man will hear and increase learning, and a man of understanding will attain wise counsel.*

*Proverbs 1:5 NKJV*

If you find yourself caught up in the inevitable challenges of these turbulent times, it's probably the right time to start searching for knowledgeable friends and mentors who can give you solid advice. Why do you need help evaluating the person in the mirror? Because you're simply too close to that person, that's why. Sometimes, you'll be tempted to give yourself straight A's when you deserve considerably lower grades. On other occasions, you'll become your own worst critic, giving yourself a string of failing marks when you deserve better. The truth, of course, is often somewhere in the middle.

Finding a wise mentor is only half the battle. It takes just as much wisdom—and sometimes more—to act upon good advice as it does to give it. So find people you can trust, listen to them carefully, and act accordingly.

It takes a wise person to give good advice, but an even wiser person to take it.

*Marie T. Freeman*

God guides through the counsel of good people.

*E. Stanley Jones*

Yes, the Spirit was sent to be our Counselor. Yes, Jesus speaks to us personally. But often he works through another human being.

*John Eldredge*

A single word, if spoken in a friendly spirit, may be sufficient to turn one from dangerous error.

*Fanny Crosby*

## Today's Prayer

*Dear Lord, thank You for the mentors whom You have placed along my path. When I am troubled, let me turn to them for help, for guidance, for comfort, and for perspective. And Father, let me be a friend and mentor to others, so that my love for You may be demonstrated by my genuine concern for them. Amen*

# Guard Your Heart and Mind

*Finally, brethren, whatever things are true, whatever things are noble, whatever things are just, whatever things are pure, whatever things are lovely, whatever things are of good report, if there is any virtue and if there is anything praiseworthy— meditate on these things.*

*Philippians 4:8 NKJV*

You are near and dear to God. He loves you more than you can imagine, and He wants the very best for you. And one more thing: God wants you to guard your heart.

Every day, you are faced with choices . . . more choices than you can count. You can do the right thing, or not. You can be prudent, or not. You can be kind, and generous, and obedient to God. Or not.

Today, the world will offer you countless opportunities to let down your guard and, by doing so, make needless mistakes that may injure you or your loved ones. So be watchful and obedient. Guard your heart by giving it to your Heavenly Father; it is safe with Him.

Becoming pure is a process of spiritual growth, and taking seriously the confession of sin during prayer time moves that process along, causing us to purge our life of practices that displease God.

*Elizabeth George*

Holiness has never been the driving force of the majority. It is, however, mandatory for anyone who wants to enter the kingdom.

*Elisabeth Elliot*

Have your heart right with Christ, and he will visit you often, and so turn weekdays into Sundays, meals into sacraments, homes into temples, and earth into heaven.

*C. H. Spurgeon*

If all struggles and sufferings were eliminated, the spirit would no more reach maturity than would the child.

*Elisabeth Elliot*

## Today's Prayer

*Dear Lord, I will guard my heart against the evils, the temptations, and the distractions of this world. I will focus, instead, upon Your love, Your blessings, and Your Son. Amen*

# Seeking God and Finding Happiness

*But happy are those . . . whose hope is in the LORD their God.*

*Psalm 146:5 NLT*

Do you sincerely want to be a happy Christian? Then set your mind and your heart upon God's love and His grace.

Happiness depends less upon our circumstances than upon our thoughts. When we turn our thoughts to God, to His gifts, and to His glorious creation, we experience the joy that God intends for His children. But, when we focus on the negative aspects of life, we suffer needlessly.

The fullness of life in Christ is available to all who seek it and claim it. Count yourself among that number. Seek first the salvation that is available through a personal relationship with Jesus Christ, and then claim the joy, the peace, and the spiritual abundance that the Shepherd offers His sheep.

God has charged Himself with full responsibility for our eternal happiness and stands ready to take over the management of our lives the moment we turn in faith to Him.

*A. W. Tozer*

Christ is the secret, the source, the substance, the center, and the circumference of all true and lasting gladness.

*Mrs. Charles E. Cowman*

Pleasure-seeking is a barren business; happiness is never found till we have the grace to stop looking for it and to give our attention to persons and matters external to ourselves.

*J. I. Packer*

No matter how hard he searches, nothing beneath the skies and nothing above the skies can make any man happy apart from God.

*C. H. Spurgeon*

## Today's Prayer

*Dear Lord, I am thankful for all the blessings You have given me. Let me be a happy Christian, Father, as I share Your joy with friends, with family, and with the world. Amen*

# Beyond Envy

*Therefore, laying aside all malice, all deceit, hypocrisy, envy, and all evil speaking, as newborn babes, desire the pure milk of the word, that you may grow thereby.*

*1 Peter 2:1-2 NKJV*

Because we are frail, imperfect human beings, we are sometimes envious of others. But God's Word warns us that envy is sin. Thus, we must guard ourselves against the natural tendency to feel resentment and jealousy when other people experience good fortune. As believers, we have absolutely no reason to be envious of any people on earth. After all, as Christians we are already recipients of the greatest gift in all creation: God's grace. We have been promised the gift of eternal life through God's only begotten Son, and we must count that gift as our most precious possession.

So here's a simple suggestion that is guaranteed to bring you happiness: fill your heart with God's love, God's promises, and God's Son . . . and when you do so, leave no room for envy, hatred, bitterness, or regret.

How can you possess the miseries of envy when you possess in Christ the best of all portions?

*C. H. Spurgeon*

To love involves trusting the beloved beyond the evidence, even against much evidence. No man is our friend who believes in our good intentions only when they are proved. No man is our friend who will not be very slow to accept evidence against them. Such confidence, between one man and another, is in fact almost universally praised as a mortal beauty, not blamed as a logical error. And the suspicious man is blamed for a meanness of character, not admired for the excellence of his logic.

*C. S. Lewis*

What God asks, does, or requires of others is not my business; it is His.

*Kay Arthur*

## Today's Prayer

*Dear Lord, when I am envious of others, redirect my thoughts to the blessings I have received from You. Make me a thankful Christian, Father, and deliver me from envy. Amen*

# We Are All Role Models

*You are the light that gives light to the world. In the same way, you should be a light for other people. Live so that they will see the good things you do and will praise your Father in heaven.*

Matthew 5:14, 16 NCV

Whether we like it or not, we are role models. Hopefully, the lives we lead and the choices we make will serve as enduring examples of the spiritual abundance that is available to all who worship God and obey His commandments.

Ask yourself this question: Are you the kind of role model that you would want to emulate? If so, congratulations. But if certain aspects of your behavior could stand improvement, the best day to begin your self-improvement regimen is this one. Because whether you realize it or not, people you love are watching your behavior, and they're learning how to live. You owe it to them—and to yourself—to live righteously and well.

A man ought to live so that everybody knows he is a Christian, and most of all, his family ought to know.

*D. L. Moody*

Your light is the truth of the Gospel message itself as well as your witness as to Who Jesus is and what He has done for you. Don't hide it.

*Anne Graham Lotz*

Our walk counts far more than our talk, always!

*George Mueller*

Living life with a consistent spiritual walk deeply influences those we love most.

*Vonette Bright*

## Today's Prayer

*Dear Lord, help me be a honorable role model to others. Let the things that I say and the things that I do show everyone what it means to be a follower of Your Son. Amen*

# Trust God's Promises and Never Lose Hope

*For you need endurance, so that after you have done God's will, you may receive what was promised.*

Hebrews 10:36 HCSB

What do you expect from the day ahead? Are you willing to trust God completely, or are you living beneath a cloud of doubt and fear? God's Word makes it clear: you should trust Him and His promises, and when you do, you can live courageously.

For thoughtful Christians, every day begins and ends with God's Son and God's promises. When we accept Christ into our hearts, God promises us the opportunity for earthly peace and spiritual abundance. But more importantly, God promises us the priceless gift of eternal life.

Sometimes, especially when we find ourselves caught in the inevitable entanglements of life, we fail to trust God completely.

Are you tired? Discouraged? Fearful? Be comforted and trust the promises that God has made to you. Are you worried or stressed? Be confident in God's power. Do you see a difficult future ahead? Be courageous and call upon God. He will protect you and then use you according to His purposes. Are you confused? Listen to the quiet voice of your Heavenly Father. He is not a God of confusion. Talk with Him; listen to Him; trust Him, and trust His promises. He is steadfast, and He is your protector . . . forever.

---

The promises of Scripture are not mere pious hopes or sanctified guesses. They are more than sentimental words to be printed on decorated cards for Sunday School children. They are eternal verities. They are true. There is no perhaps about them.

*Peter Marshall*

Only believe, don't fear. Our Master, Jesus, always watches over us, and no matter what the persecution, Jesus will surely overcome it.

*Lottie Moon*

## Today's Prayer

*Lord, Your Holy Word contains promises, and I will trust them. I will use the Bible as my guide, and I will trust You, Lord, to speak to me through Your Holy Spirit and through Your Holy Word, this day and forever. Amen*

# Make Peace with the Past

*Peace I leave with you, my peace I give unto you: not as the world giveth, give I unto you. Let not your heart be troubled, neither let it be afraid.*

John 14:27 KJV

Some of life's greatest roadblocks are not the ones we see through the windshield; they are, instead, the roadblocks that seem to fill the rearview mirror. Because we are imperfect human beings who lack perfect control over our thoughts, we may allow ourselves to become "stuck" in the past—even though we know better. Instead of focusing our thoughts and energies on the opportunities of today, we may allow painful memories to fill our minds and sap our strength. We simply can't seem to let go of our pain, so we relive it again and again . . . with predictably unfortunate consequences. Thankfully, God has other plans.

Philippians 3:13-14 instructs us to focus on the future, not the past: "One thing I do, forgetting those things which are behind and reaching forward to those things which are ahead, I press toward the goal for the prize of the upward call of God in Christ Jesus" (NKJV). Yet for many of us, focusing on the future is difficult indeed. Why? Part of the problem has to do with forgiveness. When we find ourselves focusing too intently on the past, it's a sure sign that we need to focus, instead, on a more urgent need: the need to forgive. We must thoroughly and completely forgive those who have hurt us—and we must completely forgive ourselves, too.

Can you summon both the courage and the wisdom to accept your past and move on with your life? Can you accept the reality that yesterday—and all the yesterdays before it—are gone? And, can you entrust all those yesterdays to God? Hopefully you can.

So if you've endured a difficult past, learn from it, but don't live in it. Instead, build your future on a firm foundation of trust and forgiveness: trust in your Heavenly Father, and forgiveness for all His children, including yourself.

---

Shake the dust from your past, and move forward in His promises.

*Kay Arthur*

## Today's Prayer

*Heavenly Father, free me from anger, resentment, and envy. When I am bitter, I cannot feel the peace that You intend for my life. Keep me mindful that forgiveness is Your commandment, and help me accept the past, treasure the present, and trust the future . . . to You. Amen*

# Day 47

## Seek Fellowship

*Then all the people began to eat and drink, send portions, and have a great celebration, because they had understood the words that were explained to them.*

*Nehemiah 8:12 HCSB*

Fellowship with other believers should be an integral part of your everyday life. Your association with fellow Christians should be uplifting, enlightening, encouraging, and consistent.

Are you an active member of your own fellowship? Are you a builder of bridges inside the four walls of your church and outside it? Do you contribute to God's glory by contributing your time and your talents to a close-knit band of believers? Hopefully so. The fellowship of believers is intended to be a powerful tool for spreading God's Good News and uplifting His children. And God intends for you to be a fully contributing member of that fellowship. Your intentions should be the same.

Be united with other Christians. A wall with loose bricks is not good. The bricks must be cemented together.

*Corrie ten Boom*

Christian brotherhood is not an ideal which we must realize; it is rather a reality created by God in Christ in which we may participate.

*Dietrich Bonhoeffer*

In God's economy you will be hard-pressed to find many examples of successful "Lone Rangers."

*Luci Swindoll*

When many men rejoice together, there is a richer job in each individual, since they enkindle themselves and they inflame one another.

*St. Augustine*

## Today's Prayer

*Heavenly Father, You have given me a community of supporters called the church. Let our fellowship be a reflection of the love we feel for each other and the love we feel for You. Amen*

# Keep Praying

*Is anyone among you suffering? He should pray. Is anyone cheerful? He should sing praises.*

James 5:13 HCSB

God is trying to get His message through . . . to you! Are you listening?

Perhaps, if you're experiencing tough times or uncertain times, you may find yourself overwhelmed by the press of everyday life. Perhaps you may forget to slow yourself down long enough to talk with God. Instead of turning your thoughts and prayers to Him, you may rely upon our own resources. Instead of asking God for guidance, you may depend only upon your own limited wisdom. A far better course of action is this: simply stop what you're doing long enough to open your heart to God; then listen carefully for His directions.

Do you spend time each day with God? You should. Are you in need? Ask God to sustain you. Are you troubled? Take your worries to Him in prayer. Are you weary? Seek God's strength. In all things great and small, seek God's wisdom and His grace. He hears your prayers, and He will answer. All you must do is ask.

I have found the perfect antidote for fear. Whenever it sticks up its ugly face, I clobber it with prayer.

*Dale Evans Rogers*


God always answers the prayers of His children—but His answer isn't always "Yes."

*Billy Graham*


Prayer accomplishes more than anything else.

*Bill Bright*


I have witnessed many attitudes make a positive turnaround through prayer.

*John Maxwell*


## Today's Prayer

*Dear Lord, let me raise my hopes and my dreams, my worries and my fears to You. Let me be a worthy example to family and friends, showing them the importance and the power of prayer. Let me take everything to You in prayer, Lord, and when I do, let me trust in Your answers. Amen*

# Walking in His Footsteps

*I've laid down a pattern for you. What I've done, you do.*

John 13:15 MSG

As citizens of a fast-changing world, we face challenges that sometimes leave us feeling overworked, overcommitted, and overwhelmed. But God has different plans for us. He intends that we slow down long enough to praise Him and to glorify His Son.

Each day, we are confronted with countless opportunities to serve God and to follow in the footsteps of His Son. When we do, our Heavenly Father guides our steps and blesses our endeavors. He lifts our spirits and enriches our lives.

Today provides a glorious opportunity to place yourself in the service of the One who is the Giver of all blessings. May you seek His will, may you trust His Word, and may you walk in the footsteps of His Son.

Christ is to be sought and bought with any pains, at any price; we cannot buy this gold too dear. He is a jewel worth more than a thousand worlds. Get him, and get all; miss him and miss all.

*Thomas Brooks*

To walk out of His will is to walk into nowhere.

*C. S. Lewis*

Imagine the spiritual strength the disciples drew from walking hundreds of miles with Jesus . . . (3 John 4).

*Jim Maxwell*

WWJD = Walking With Jesus Daily.

*Anonymous*

## Today's Prayer

*Dear Jesus, because I am Your disciple, I will trust You, I will obey Your teachings, and I will share Your Good News. You have given me life abundant and life eternal, and I will follow You today and forever. Amen*

# Finding Real Fulfillment

*For You, O God, have tested us; You have refined us as silver is refined . . . we went through fire and through water; but You brought us out to rich fulfillment.*

Psalm 66:10–12 NKJV

Everywhere we turn, or so it seems, the world promises fulfillment, contentment, and happiness. But the contentment that the world offers is fleeting and incomplete. Thankfully, the fulfillment that God offers is all encompassing and everlasting.

Sometimes, amid the inevitable hustle and bustle of life, we can forfeit—albeit temporarily—the joy of Christ as we wrestle with the challenges of daily living. Yet God's Word is clear: fulfillment through Christ is available to all who seek it and claim it. Count yourself among that number. Seek first a personal, transforming relationship with Jesus, and then claim the joy, the fulfillment, and the spiritual abundance that the Shepherd offers His sheep.

Find satisfaction in him who made you, and only then find satisfaction in yourself as part of his creation.

*St. Augustine*

We are never more fulfilled than when our longing for God is met by His presence in our lives.

*Billy Graham*

We are made for God, and nothing less will really satisfy us.

*Brennan Manning*

Our sense of joy, satisfaction, and fulfillment in life increases, no matter what the circumstances, if we are in the center of God's will.

*Billy Graham*

## Today's Prayer

*Dear Lord, when I turn my thoughts and prayers to You, I feel peace and fulfillment. But sometimes, when I am distracted by the busyness of the day, fulfillment seems far away. Today, let me trust Your will, let me follow Your commands, and let me accept Your peace. Amen*

# Focusing Your Thoughts

*Let your eyes look forward; fix your gaze straight ahead.*

*Proverbs 4:25 HCSB*

This day—and every day hereafter—is a chance to celebrate the life that God has given you. It's also a chance to give thanks to the One who has offered you more blessings than you can possibly count. What is your focus today? Are you willing to focus your thoughts and energies on God's blessings and upon His will for your life? Or will you turn your thoughts to other things?

Today, why not focus your thoughts on the joy that is rightfully yours in Christ? Why not take time to celebrate God's glorious creation? Why not trust your hopes instead of your fears? When you do, you will think optimistically about yourself and your world . . . and you can then share your optimism with others. They'll be better for it, and so will you. But not necessarily in that order.

Measure the size of the obstacles against the size of God.

*Beth Moore*

We need to stop focusing on our lacks and stop giving out excuses and start looking at and listening to Jesus.

*Anne Graham Lotz*

What is your focus today? Joy comes when it is Jesus first, others second…then you.

*Kay Arthur*

Don't let worry rob you of the joy that is rightfully yours. God is in heaven, and He knows your every need. Focus on God and His provisions, and watch gratefully as the worries of today begin to fade away.

*Marie T. Freeman*

## Today's Prayer

*Dear Lord, help me to face this day with a spirit of optimism and thanksgiving. And let me focus my thoughts on You and Your incomparable gifts. Amen*

# Day 52

# He's Right Here, Right Now

*The Lord is with you when you are with Him. If you seek Him, He will be found by you.*

2 Chronicles 15:2 HCSB

Since God is everywhere, we are free to sense His presence whenever we take the time to quiet our souls and turn our prayers to Him. But sometimes, amid the incessant demands of everyday life, we turn our thoughts far from God; when we do, we suffer.

Do you set aside quiet moments each day to offer praise to your Creator? As a person who has received the gift of God's grace, you most certainly should. Silence is a gift that you give to yourself and to God. During these moments of stillness, you will often sense the infinite love and power of your Creator—and He, in turn, will speak directly to your heart.

The familiar words of Psalm 46:10 remind us to "Be still, and know that I am God." When we do so, we encounter the awesome presence of our loving Heavenly Father, and we are comforted in the knowledge that God is not just near. He is here.

God is in the midst of whatever has happened, is happening, and will happen.

*Charles Swindoll*

Our souls were made to live in an upper atmosphere, and we stifle and choke if we live on any lower level. Our eyes were made to look off from these heavenly heights, and our vision is distorted by any lower gazing.

*Hannah Whitall Smith*

Through the death and broken body of Jesus Christ on the Cross, you and I have been given access to the presence of God when we approach Him by faith in prayer.

*Anne Graham Lotz*

## Today's Prayer

*Heavenly Father, help me to feel Your presence in every situation and every circumstance. You are with me, Lord, in times of celebration and in times of sorrow. You are with me when I am strong and when I am weak. You never leave my side even when it seems to me that You are far away. Today and every day, God, let me feel You and acknowledge Your presence so that others, too, might know You through me. Amen*

# Day 53

## Discovering God's Plans

*It is God who is at work in you, both to will and to work for His good pleasure.*

*Philippians 2:13 NASB*

If you seek to live in accordance with God's will for your life—and you should—then you will live in accordance with His commandments. You will study God's Word, and you will be watchful for His signs. You will associate with fellow Christians who will encourage your spiritual growth, and you will listen to that inner voice that speaks to you in the quiet moments of your daily devotionals.

God intends to use you in wonderful, unexpected ways if you let Him. The decision to seek God's plan and to follow it is yours and yours alone. The consequences of that decision have implications that are both profound and eternal, so choose carefully.

God has plans—not problems—for our lives. Before she died in the concentration camp in Ravensbruck, my sister Betsie said to me, "Corrie, your whole life has been a training for the work you are doing here in prison— and for the work you will do afterward."

*Corrie ten Boom*

God has a plan for the life of every Christian. Every circumstance, every turn of destiny, all things work together for your good and for His glory.

*Billy Graham*

Let's never forget that some of God's greatest mercies are His refusals. He says no in order that He may, in some way we cannot imagine, say yes. All His ways with us are merciful. His meaning is always love.

*Elisabeth Elliot*

## Today's Prayer

*Dear Lord, You created me for a reason. Give me the wisdom to follow Your direction for my life's journey. Let me do Your work here on earth by seeking Your will and living it, knowing that when I trust in You, Father, I am eternally blessed. Amen*

# Beyond Failure

*For a righteous man may fall seven times and rise again.*

*Proverbs 24:16 NKJV*

The occasional disappointments and failures of life are inevitable. Such setbacks are simply the price that we must occasionally pay for our willingness to take risks as we follow our dreams. But even when we encounter bitter disappointments, we must never lose faith.

When we encounter the inevitable difficulties of life, God stands ready to protect us. Our responsibility, of course, is to ask Him for protection. When we call upon Him in heartfelt prayer, He will answer—in His own time and according to His own plan—and He will heal us. And, while we are waiting for God's plans to unfold and for His healing touch to restore us, we can be comforted in the knowledge that our Creator can overcome any obstacle, even if we cannot.

The almighty Father will use life's reverses to move you forward.

*Barbara Johnson*

The enemy of our souls loves to taunt us with past failures, wrongs, disappointments, disasters, and calamities. And if we let him continue doing this, our life becomes a long and dark tunnel, with very little light at the end.

*Charles Swindoll*

God is a specialist; He is well able to work our failures into His plans. Often the doorway to success is entered through the hallway of failure.

*Erwin Lutzer*

God sometimes permits us to experience humiliating defeats in order to test our faith and to reveal to us what's really going on in our hearts.

*Warren Wiersbe*

## Today's Prayer

*Dear Lord, even when I'm afraid of failure, give me the courage to try. Remind me that with You by my side, I really have nothing to fear. So today, Father, I will live courageously as I place my faith in You. Amen*

# God Is Love

*God is love; and he that dwelleth in love dwelleth in God, and God in him.*

*1 John 4:16 KJV*

The Bible makes this promise: God is love. It's a sweeping statement, a profoundly important description of what God is and how God works. God's love is perfect. When we open our hearts to His perfect love, we are touched by the Creator's hand, and we are transformed.

Today, even if you can only carve out a few quiet moments, offer sincere prayers of thanksgiving to your Creator. He loves you now and throughout all eternity. Open your heart to His presence and His love.

The greatest love of all is God's love for us, a love that showed itself in action.

*Billy Graham*

The life of faith is a daily exploration of the constant and countless ways in which God's grace and love are experienced.

*Eugene Peterson*

Love, for instance, is not something God has which may grow or diminish or cease to be. His love is the way God is, and when He loves He is simply being Himself.

*A. W. Tozer*

If it is maintained that anything so small as the Earth must, in any event, be too unimportant to merit the love of the Creator, we reply that no Christian ever supposed we did merit it. Christ did not die for men because they were intrinsically worth dying for, but because He is intrinsically love, and therefore loves infinitely.

*C. S. Lewis*

## Today's Prayer

*Dear God, You are love. You love me, Father, and I love You. As I love You more, Lord, I am also able to love my family and friends more. I will be Your loving servant, Lord, today and throughout eternity. Amen*

# Using God's Gifts

*Based on the gift they have received, everyone should use it
to serve others, as good managers of the varied grace of God.*

*1 Peter 4:10 HCSB*

The gifts that you possess are gifts from the Giver of all things good. Do you have a spiritual gift? Share it. Do you have a testimony about the things that Christ has done for you? Don't leave your story untold. Do you possess financial resources? Share them. Do you have particular talents? Hone your skills and use them for God's glory.

When you hoard the treasures that God has given you, you live in rebellion against His commandments. But, when you obey God by sharing His gifts freely and without fanfare, you invite Him to bless you more and more. Today, be a faithful steward of your talents and treasures. And then prepare yourself for even greater blessings that are sure to come.

When God crowns our merits, he is crowning nothing other than his gifts.

*St. Augustine*

God is still in the process of dispensing gifts, and He uses ordinary individuals like us to develop those gifts in other people.

*Howard Hendricks*

If I find in myself a desire which no experience in this world can satisfy, the most probable explanation is that I was made for another world.

*C. S. Lewis*

There's a unique sense of fulfillment that comes when we submit our gifts to God's use and ask him to energize them in a supernatural way—and then step back to watch what he does. It can be the difference between merely existing in black and white and living a life in full, brilliant color.

*Lee Strobel*

## Today's Prayer

*Dear Lord, let me use my gifts, and let me help my friends and family discover theirs. Your gifts are priceless and eternal. May we, Your children, use them to the glory of Your kingdom, today and forever. Amen*

# Neighbors in Need

*Each one of us needs to look after the good of the people around us, asking ourselves, "How can I help?" That's exactly what Jesus did.*

Romans 15:2-3 MSG

Neighbors. We know that we are instructed to love them, and yet there's so little time…and we're so busy. No matter. As Christians, we are commanded by our Lord and Savior Jesus Christ to love our neighbors just as we love ourselves. Period.

This very day, you will encounter someone who needs a word of encouragement, or a pat on the back, or a helping hand, or a heartfelt prayer. And, if you don't reach out to your friend, who will? If you don't take the time to understand the needs of your neighbors, who will? If you don't love your brothers and sisters, who will? So, today, look for a neighbor in need…and then do something to help. Father's orders.

The truest help we can render an afflicted man is not to take his burden from him, but to call out his best energy, that he may be able to bear the burden himself.

*Phillips Brooks*

Make it a rule, and pray to God to help you to keep it, never, if possible, to lie down at night without being able to say: "I have made one human being at least a little wiser, or a little happier, or at least a little better this day."

*Charles Kingsley*

Encouraging others means helping people, looking for the best in them, and trying to bring out their positive qualities.

*John Maxwell*

Do all the good you can. By all the means you can. In all the ways you can. In all the places you can. At all the times you can. To all the people you can. As long as ever you can.

*John Wesley*

## Today's Prayer

*Heavenly Father, help me be a Good Samaritan to the people You place along my path, today and every day. Amen*

# Honoring God

*Honor GOD with everything you own; give him the first and the best. Your barns will burst, your wine vats will brim over.*

Proverbs 3:9-10 MSG

At times, your life is probably hectic, demanding, and complicated. When the demands of life leave you rushing from place to place with scarcely a moment to spare, you may fail to pause and thank your Creator for the blessings He has bestowed upon you. But that's a big mistake.

Whom will you choose to honor today? If you honor God and place Him at the center of your life, every day is a cause for celebration. But if you fail to honor your Heavenly Father, you're asking for trouble, and lots of it. So honor God for who He is and for what He has done for you. And don't just honor Him on Sunday morning. Praise Him all day long, every day, for as long as you live . . . and then for all eternity.

God shows unbridled delight when He sees people acting in ways that honor Him.

*Bill Hybels*

We honor God by asking for great things when they are a part of His promise. We dishonor Him and cheat ourselves when we ask for molehills where He has promised mountains.

*Vance Havner*

What lessons about honor did you learn from your childhood? Are you living what you learned today?

*Dennis Swanberg*

Happiness is to be found only in the home where God is loved and honored, where each one loves, and helps, and cares for the others.

*St. Theophane Venard*

## Today's Prayer

*I praise You, Lord, from the depths of my heart, and I give thanks for Your goodness, for Your mercy, and for Your Son. Let me honor You every day of my life through my words and my deeds. Let me honor You, Father, with all that I am. Amen*

# Finding Hope

*You, Lord, give true peace to those who depend on you, because they trust you.*

*Isaiah 26:3 NCV*

Sometimes, hope is a perishable commodity. Despite God's promises, despite Christ's love, and despite our countless blessings, we frail human beings can still lose hope from time to time. When the challenges and pressures of everyday life threaten to overwhelm us, we may convince ourselves that the future holds little promise—and we may allow our fears to eclipse our dreams.

When hope seems to be in short supply, there is a source to which we can turn in order to restore our perspective and our strength. That source is God. When we lift our prayers to the Creator, we avail ourselves of God's power, God's wisdom, and God's love. And when we allow God's Son to reign over our hearts, we are transformed, not just for a day, but for all eternity.

Are you looking for a renewed sense of hope? If so, it's time to place your future in the loving hands of God's only begotten Son. When you do, you'll discover that hope is not only highly perishable, but that it is also readily renewable . . . one day—and one moment—at a time.

Never yield to gloomy anticipation. Place your hope and confidence in God. He has no record of failure.

*Mrs. Charles E. Cowman*

Without the certainty of His resurrection, we would come to the end of this life without hope, with nothing to anticipate except despair and doubt. But because He lives, we rejoice, knowing soon we will meet our Savior face to face, and the troubles and trials of this world will be behind us.

*Bill Bright*

Oh, remember this: There is never a time when we may not hope in God. Whatever our necessities, however great our difficulties, and though to all appearance help is impossible, yet our business is to hope in God, and it will be found that it is not in vain.

*George Mueller*

## Today's Prayer

*Dear Lord, I will place my hope in You. If I become discouraged, I will turn to You. If I am afraid, I will seek strength in You. In every aspect of my life, I will trust You. You are my Father, and I will place my hope, my trust, and my faith in You. Amen*

# Contagious Faith

*So roll up your sleeves, put your mind in gear, be totally ready to receive the gift that's coming when Jesus arrives. Don't lazily slip back into those old grooves of evil, doing just what you feel like doing. You didn't know any better then; you do now. As obedient children, let yourselves be pulled into a way of life shaped by God's life, a life energetic and blazing with holiness.*

1 Peter 1:13-15 MSG

Are you genuinely excited about your faith? And do you make your enthusiasm known to those around you? Or are you a "silent ambassador" for Christ? God's preference is clear: He intends that you stand before others and proclaim your faith.

Genuine, heartfelt Christianity is contagious. If you enjoy a life-altering relationship with God, that relationship will have an impact on others—perhaps a profound impact.

Does Christ reign over your life? Then share your testimony and your excitement. The world needs both.

Prayer must be aflame. Prayer without fervor is as a sun without light or heat, or as a flower without beauty or fragrance. A soul devoted to God is a fervent soul, and prayer is the creature of that flame. He only can truly pray who is all aglow for holiness, for God, and for heaven.

*E. M. Bounds*

Living life with a consistent spiritual walk deeply influences those we love most.

*Vonette Bright*

Catch on fire with enthusiasm and people will come for miles to watch you burn.

*John Wesley*

Don't take hold of a thing unless you want that thing to take hold of you.

*E. Stanley Jones*

## Today's Prayer

*Dear Lord, I know that others are watching the way that I live my life. Help me to be an enthusiastic Christian with a faith that is contagious. Amen.*

# The Struggle Against Worldliness

*And do not be conformed to this world, but be transformed by the renewing of your mind, so that you may prove what the will of God is, that which is good and acceptable and perfect.*

*Romans 12:2 NASB*

We live in the world, but we should not worship it—yet at every turn, or so it seems, we are tempted to do otherwise. As Warren Wiersbe correctly observed, "Because the world is deceptive, it is dangerous."

The 21st-century world we live in is a noisy, stress-filled, distracting place, a place that offers countless temptations and dangers. The world seems to cry, "Worship me with your time, your money, your energy, your thoughts, and your life!" But if we are wise, we won't fall prey to that temptation.

C. S. Lewis said, "Aim at heaven and you will get earth thrown in; aim at earth and you will get neither." That's good advice. You're likely to hit what you aim at, so aim high . . . aim at heaven.

Our fight is not against any physical enemy; it is against organizations and powers that are spiritual. We must struggle against sin all our lives, but we are assured we will win.

*Corrie ten Boom*

The more we stuff ourselves with material pleasures, the less we seem to appreciate life.

*Barbara Johnson*

All those who look to draw their satisfaction from the wells of the world—pleasure, popularity, position, possessions, politics, power, prestige, finances, family, friends, fame, fortune, career, children, church, clubs, sports, sex, success, recognition, reputation, religion, education, entertainment, exercise, honors, health, hobbies—will soon be thirsty again!

*Anne Graham Lotz*

## Today's Prayer

*Lord, this world is a crazy place, and I have many opportunities to stray from Your commandments. Help me to obey You! Let me keep Christ in my heart, and let me put the devil in his place: far away from me! Amen*

# Experiencing Silence

*Be still, and know that I am God.*

*Psalm 46:10 NKJV*

The world seems to grow louder day by day, and our senses seem to be invaded at every turn. If we allow the distractions of a clamorous society to separate us from God's peace, we do ourselves a profound disservice. Our task, as dutiful believers, is to carve out moments of silence in a world filled with noise.

If we are to maintain righteous minds and compassionate hearts, we must take time each day for prayer and for meditation. We must make ourselves still in the presence of our Creator. We must quiet our minds and our hearts so that we might sense God's will and His love.

Has the busy pace of life robbed you of the peace that God has promised? If so, it's time to reorder your priorities and your life. Nothing is more important than the time you spend with your Heavenly Father. So be still and claim the inner peace that is found in the silent moments you spend with God.

Let your loneliness be transformed into a holy aloneness. Sit still before the Lord. Remember Naomi's word to Ruth: "Sit still, my daughter, until you see how the matter will fall."

*Elisabeth Elliot*

Because Jesus Christ is our Great High Priest, not only can we approach God without a human "go-between," we can also hear and learn from God in some sacred moments without one.

*Beth Moore*

In the soul-searching of our lives, we are to stay quiet so we can hear Him say all that He wants to say to us in our hearts.

*Charles Swindoll*

It is in that stillness that the Voice will be heard, the only voice in all the universe that speaks peace to the deepest part of us.

*Elisabeth Elliot*

## Today's Prayer

*Dear Lord, help me remember the importance of silence. Help me discover quiet moments throughout the day so that I can sense Your presence and Your love. Amen*

# Answering the Call

*I urge you now to live the life to which God called you.*

*Ephesians 4:1 NKJV*

God is calling you to follow a specific path that He has chosen for your life. And it is vitally important that you heed that call. Otherwise, your talents and opportunities may go unused.

Have you already heard God's call? And are you pursuing it with vigor? If so, you're both fortunate and wise. But if you have not yet discovered what God intends for you to do with your life, keep searching and keep praying until you discover why the Creator put you here.

Remember: God has important work for you to do—work that no one else on earth can accomplish but you. The Creator has placed you in a particular location, amid particular people, with unique opportunities to serve. And He has given you all the tools you need to succeed. So listen for His voice, watch for His signs, and prepare yourself for the call that is sure to come.

If God has called you, do not spend time looking over your shoulder to see who is following you.

*Corrie ten Boom*

He treats us as sons, and all he asks in return is that we shall treat Him as a Father whom we can trust without anxiety. We must take the son's place of dependence and trust, and we must let Him keep the father's place of care and responsibility.

*Hannah Whitall Smith*

When you become consumed by God's call on your life, everything will take on new meaning and significance. You will begin to see every facet of your life, including your pain, as a means through which God can work to bring others to Himself.

*Charles Stanley*

## Today's Prayer

*Heavenly Father, You have called me, and I acknowledge that calling. In these quiet moments before this busy day unfolds, I come to You. I will study Your Word and seek Your guidance. Give me the wisdom to know Your will for my life and the courage to follow wherever You may lead me, today and forever. Amen*

# Choosing to Be Generous

*Each person should do as he has decided in his heart—not out of regret or out of necessity, for God loves a cheerful giver.*

2 Corinthians 9:7 HCSB

When you give generously to those who need your help, God will bless your endeavors and enrich your life. So, if you're looking for a surefire way to improve the quality of your day or your life, here it is: find ways to share your blessings.

God rewards generosity just as surely as He punishes sin. If we become generous disciples in the service of our Lord, God blesses us in ways that we cannot fully understand. But if we allow ourselves to become close-fisted and miserly, either with our possessions or with our love, we deprive ourselves of the spiritual abundance that would otherwise be ours.

Do you seek God's abundance and His peace? Then share the blessings that God has given you. Share your possessions, share your faith, share your testimony, and share your love. God expects no less, and He deserves no less. And neither, come to think of it, do your neighbors.

If you want to be truly happy, you won't find it on an endless quest for more stuff. You'll find it in receiving God's generosity and in passing that generosity along.

*Bill Hybels*

The measure of a life, after all, is not its duration but its donation.

*Corrie ten Boom*

As faithful stewards of what we have, ought we not to give earnest thought to our staggering surplus?

*Elisabeth Elliot*

What is your focus today? Joy comes when it is Jesus first, others second . . . then you.

*Kay Arthur*

## Today's Prayer

*Dear Lord, Your Word tells me that it is more blessed to give than to receive. Make me a faithful steward of the gifts You have given me, and let me share those gifts generously with others, today and every day that I live. Amen*

# We Belong to Him

*Now return to the LORD your God, for He is gracious and compassionate, slow to anger, abounding in lovingkindness.*

*Joel 2:13 NASB*

The line from the children's song is reassuring and familiar: "Little ones to Him belong. We are weak but He is strong." That message applies to kids of all ages: we are all indeed weak, but we worship a mighty God who meets our needs and answers our prayers.

Are you in the midst of adversity or in the grips of temptation? If so, turn to God for strength. The Bible promises that you can do all things through the power of our risen Savior, Jesus Christ. Your challenge, then, is clear: you must place Christ where He belongs: at the very center of your life. When you do, you will discover that, yes, Jesus loves you and that, yes, He will give you direction and strength if you ask it in His name.

Our hearts have been made to cry out for a love that can come only from our Creator.

*Angela Thomas*

God knows all that is true about us and is a friend to the face we show and the face we hide. He does not love us less for our human weaknesses.

*Sheila Walsh*

God loves me as God loves all people, without qualification. To be in the image of God means that all of us are made for the purpose of knowing and loving God and one another and of being loved in turn, not literally in the same way God knows and loves, but in a way appropriate to human beings.

*Roberta Bondi*

## Today's Prayer

*Thank You, Lord, for Your love. Your love is boundless, infinite, and eternal. Today, as I pause and reflect upon Your love for me, let me share that love with all those who cross my path. And, as an expression of my love for You, Father, let me share the saving message of Your Son with a world in desperate need of His hope, His peace, and His salvation. Amen*

# Finding Strength in Turbulent Times

*I can do all things through Christ who strengthens me.*

*Philippians 4:13 NKJV*

God's love and support never changes. From the cradle to the grave, God has promised to give you the strength to meet any challenge. God has promised to lift you up and guide your steps if you let Him. God has promised that when you entrust your life to Him completely and without reservation, He will give you the courage to face any trial and the wisdom to live in His righteousness.

God's hand uplifts those who turn their hearts and prayers to Him. Will you count yourself among that number? Will you accept God's peace and wear God's armor against the temptations and distractions of our dangerous world? If you do, you can live courageously and optimistically, knowing that you have been forever touched by the loving, unfailing, uplifting hand of God.

When trials come your way—as inevitably they will—do not run away. Run to your God and Father.

*Kay Arthur*

The same God who empowered Samson, Gideon, and Paul seeks to empower my life and your life, because God hasn't changed.

*Bill Hybels*

A divine strength is given to those who yield themselves to the Father and obey what He tells them to do.

*Warren Wiersbe*

One with God is a majority.

*Billy Graham*

## Today's Prayer

*Lord, sometimes life is difficult. Sometimes, I am worried, weary, or heartbroken. But, when I lift my eyes to You, Father, You strengthen me. When I am weak, You lift me up. Today, I turn to You, Lord, for my strength, for my hope, and my salvation. Amen*

# The Wisdom to Be Hopeful

*Now if any of you lacks wisdom, he should ask God, who gives to all generously and without criticizing, and it will be given to him. But let him ask in faith without doubting. For the doubter is like the surging sea, driven and tossed by the wind.*

*James 1:5-6 HCSB*

Wisdom and hope are traveling companions. Wise men and women learn to think optimistically about their lives, their futures, and their faith. The pessimists, however, are not so fortunate; they choose instead to focus their thoughts and energies on faultfinding, criticizing, and complaining, with precious little to show for their efforts.

To become wise, we must seek God's wisdom—the wisdom of hope—and we must live according to God's Word. To become wise, we must seek God's guidance with consistency and purpose. To become wise, we must not only learn the lessons of life, we must live by them.

Do you seek wisdom for yourself and for your family? Then remember this: The ultimate source of wisdom is the Word of God. When you study God's Word and live according to His commandments, you will grow wise, you will remain hopeful, and you will be a blessing to your family and to the world.

If we neglect the Bible, we cannot expect to benefit from the wisdom and direction that result from knowing God's Word.

*Vonette Bright*

The more wisdom enters our hearts, the more we will be able to trust our hearts in difficult situations.

*John Eldredge*

This is my song through endless ages: Jesus led me all the way.

*Fanny Crosby*

Wisdom is knowledge applied. Head knowledge is useless on the battlefield. Knowledge stamped on the heart makes one wise.

*Beth Moore*

## Today's Prayer

*Dear Lord, when I depend upon the world's wisdom, I make many mistakes. But when I trust in Your wisdom, I build my life on a firm foundation. Today and every day I will trust Your Word and follow it, knowing that the ultimate wisdom is Your wisdom and the ultimate truth is Your truth. Amen*

# Your Bright Future

*"For I know the plans I have for you"—[this is] the Lord's declaration—"plans for [your] welfare, not for disaster, to give you a future and a hope."*

*Jeremiah 29:11 HCSB*

How bright is your future? Well, if you're a faithful believer, God's plans for you are so bright that you'd better wear shades. But here's an important question: How bright do you believe your future to be? Are you expecting a terrific tomorrow, or are you dreading a terrible one? The answer you give will have a powerful impact on the way tomorrow turns out.

Do you trust in the ultimate goodness of God's plan for your life? Will you face tomorrow's challenges with optimism and hope? You should. After all, God created you for a very important reason: His reason. And you still have important work to do: His work.

Today, as you live in the present and look to the future, remember that God has an amazing plan for you. Act—and believe—accordingly.

That we may not complain of what is, let us see God's hand in all events; and, that we may not be afraid of what shall be, let us see all events in God's hand.

*Matthew Henry*

We spend our lives dreaming of the future, not realizing that a little of it slips away every day.

*Barbara Johnson*

Do not limit the limitless God! With Him, face the future unafraid because you are never alone.

*Mrs. Charles E. Cowman*

Every experience God gives us, every person he brings into our lives, is the perfect preparation for the future that only he can see.

*Corrie ten Boom*

## Today's Prayer

*Dear Lord, as I look to the future, I will place my trust in You. If I become discouraged, I will turn to You. If I am afraid, I will seek strength in You. You are my Father, and I will place my hope, my trust, and my faith in You. Amen*

# Character Matters

*The one who lives with integrity lives securely, but whoever perverts his ways will be found out.*

*Proverbs 10:9 HCSB*

Charles Swindoll correctly observed, "Nothing speaks louder or more powerfully than a life of integrity." Righteous men and women agree.

Character is built slowly over a lifetime. It is the sum of every right decision, every honest word, every noble thought, and every heartfelt prayer. It is forged on the anvil of honorable work and polished by the twin virtues of generosity and humility. Character is a precious thing—difficult to build but easy to tear down. As believers in Christ, we must seek to live each day with discipline, honesty, and faith. When we do, integrity becomes a habit.

Psalm 145 promises, "The Lord is near to all who call on him, to all who call on him in truth. He fulfills the desires of those who fear him; he hears their cry and saves them" (v. 18-20 NIV). And the words of Jesus offer us comfort: "These things I have spoken to you, that in Me you may have peace. In the world you will have tribulation; but be of good cheer, I have overcome the world" (John 16:33 NKJV).

The times that try your soul are also the times that build your character. During the darker days of life, you can learn lessons that are impossible to learn during sunny, happier days. Times of adversity can—and should—be times of intense spiritual and personal growth. But God will not force you to learn the lessons of adversity. You must learn them for yourself.

---

Every time you refuse to face up to life and its problems, you weaken your character.

*E. Stanley Jones*

Jesus—the standard of measurement, the scale of weights, the test of character for the whole moral universe.

*R. G. Lee*

## Today's Prayer

*Dear Lord, every day can be an exercise in character-building, and that's what I intend to make this day. I will be mindful that my thoughts and actions have great consequences, consequences in my own life and in the lives of my loved ones. I will strive to make my thoughts and actions pleasing to You, so that I may be an instrument of Your peace, today and every day. Amen*

# Open Up Your Heart

*We know that all things work together for the good of those who love God: those who are called according to His purpose.*

Romans 8:28 HCSB

C. S. Lewis observed, "A man's spiritual health is exactly proportional to his love for God." If we are to enjoy the spiritual health that God intends for us, we must praise Him, we must love Him, and we must obey Him.

When we worship God faithfully and obediently, we invite His love into our hearts. When we truly worship God, we allow Him to rule over our days and our lives. In turn, we grow to love God even more deeply as we sense His love for us.

St. Augustine wrote, "I love you, Lord, not doubtingly, but with absolute certainty. Your Word beat upon my heart until I fell in love with you, and now the universe and everything in it tells me to love you."

Today, open your heart to the Father. And let your obedience be a fitting response to His never-ending love.

Joy is a by-product not of happy circumstances, education or talent, but of a healthy relationship with God and a determination to love Him no matter what.

*Barbara Johnson*

Delighting thyself in the Lord is the sudden realization that He has become the desire of your heart.

*Beth Moore*

Loving Him means the thankful acceptance of all things that His love has appointed.

*Elisabeth Elliot*

When an honest soul can get still before the living Christ, we can still hear Him say simply and clearly, "Love the Lord your God with all your heart and with all your soul and with all your mind . . . and love one another as I have loved you."

*Gloria Gaither*

## Today's Prayer

*Dear Heavenly Father, You have blessed me with a love that is infinite and eternal. Let me love You, Lord, more and more each day. Make me a loving servant, Father, today and throughout eternity. And, let me show my love for You by sharing Your message and Your love with others. Amen*

# Consider the Possibilities

*For nothing will be impossible with God.*

*Luke 1:37 HCSB*

Are you afraid to ask God to do big things—or to make big changes—in your life? Is your faith threadbare and worn? If so, it's time to abandon your doubts and reclaim your faith in God's promises.

Ours is a God of infinite possibilities. But sometimes, because of limited faith and limited understanding, we wrongly assume that God cannot or will not intervene in the affairs of mankind. Such assumptions are simply wrong.

God's Holy Word makes it clear: absolutely nothing is impossible for the Lord. And since the Bible means what it says, you can be comforted in the knowledge that the Creator of the universe can do miraculous things in your own life and in the lives of your loved ones. Your challenge, as a believer, is to take God at His word, and to expect the miraculous.

Man's adversity is God's opportunity.

*Matthew Henry*

God specializes in things thought impossible.

*Catherine Marshall*

If all things are possible with God, then all things are possible to him who believes in him.

*Corrie ten Boom*

Do we not continually pass by blessings innumerable without notice, and instead fix our eyes on what we feel to be our trials and our losses? And, do we not think and talk about our trials until our whole horizon is filled with them, and we almost begin to think we have no blessings at all?

*Hannah Whitall Smith*

## Today's Prayer

*Dear Lord, give me the courage to dream and the faithfulness to trust in Your perfect plan for my life. When I am worried, give me strength for today and hope for tomorrow. Today, Father, I will trust You and honor You with my thoughts, with my prayers, with my actions, and with my dreams. Amen*

# God's Protection

*Though I sit in darkness, the Lord will be my light.*

*Micah 7:8 HCSB*

Have you ever faced challenges that seemed too big to handle? Have you ever faced big problems that, despite your best efforts, simply could not be solved? If so, you know how uncomfortable it is to feel helpless in the face of difficult circumstances. Thankfully, even when there's nowhere else to turn, you can turn your thoughts and prayers to God, and He will respond.

God's hand uplifts those who turn their hearts and prayers to Him. Count yourself among that number. When you do, you can live courageously and joyfully, knowing that "this too will pass"—but that God's love for you will not. And you can draw strength from the knowledge that you are a marvelous creation, loved, protected, and uplifted by the ever-present hand of God.

God helps those who help themselves, but there are times when we are quite incapable of helping ourselves. That's when God stoops down and gathers us in His arms like a mother lifts a sick child, and does for us what we cannot do for ourselves.

*Ruth Bell Graham*

Life is literally filled with God-appointed storms. These squalls surge across everyone's horizon. We all need them.

*Charles Swindoll*

God will not permit any troubles to come upon us unless He has a specific plan by which great blessing can come out of the difficulty.

*Peter Marshall*

## Today's Prayer

*Lord, sometimes life is difficult. Sometimes, I am worried, weary, or heartbroken. And sometimes, I encounter powerful temptations to disobey Your commandments. But, when I lift my eyes to You, Father, You strengthen me. When I am weak, You lift me up. Today, I will turn to You for strength, for hope, for direction, and for deliverance. Amen*

# Relying upon Him

*Therefore humble yourselves under the mighty hand of God, that He may exalt you at the proper time, casting all your anxiety on Him, because He cares for you.*

*1 Peter 5:6-7 NASB*

Do the demands of this day threaten to overwhelm you? If so, you must rely not only upon your own resources but also upon the promises of your Father in heaven.

God is a never-ending source of support and courage for those of us who call upon Him. When we are weary, He gives us strength. When we see no hope, God reminds us of His promises. When we grieve, God wipes away our tears.

God will hold your hand and walk with you every day of your life if you let Him. So even if your circumstances are difficult, trust the Father. His love is eternal and His goodness endures forever.

Faith is not merely you holding on to God—it is God holding on to you.

*E. Stanley Jones*

When you have no helpers, see all your helpers in God. When you have many helpers, see God in all your helpers. When you have nothing but God, see all in God; when you have everything, see God in everything. Under all conditions, stay thy heart only on the Lord.

*C. H. Spurgeon*

The more you give your mental burdens to the Lord, the more exciting it becomes to see how God will handle things that are impossible for you to do anything about.

*Charles Swindoll*

God uses our most stumbling, faltering faith-steps as the open door to His doing for us "more than we ask or think."

*Catherine Marshall*

## Today's Prayer

*Heavenly Father, You never leave or forsake me. You are always with me, protecting me and encouraging me. Whatever this day may bring, I thank You for Your love and Your strength. Amen*

# Giving Thanks for Christ's Love

*Your old life is dead. Your new life, which is your real life—*
*even though invisible to spectators—is with Christ in God.*
*He is your life.*

Colossians 3:3 MSG

Christ's love is perfect and steadfast. Even though we are fallible, and wayward, the Good Shepherd cares for us still. What does the love of Christ mean to His believers? It changes everything. Even though we have fallen far short of the Father's commandments, Christ loves us with a power and depth that is beyond our understanding. And, as we accept Christ's love and walk in Christ's footsteps, our lives bear testimony to His power and to His grace. Yes, Christ's love changes everything; may we invite Him into our hearts so it can then change everything in us.

Live your lives in love, the same sort of love which Christ gives us, and which He perfectly expressed when He gave Himself as a sacrifice to God.

*Corrie ten Boom*

So Jesus came, stripping himself of everything as he came—omnipotence, omniscience, omnipresence—everything except love. "He emptied himself" (Philippians 2:7), emptied himself of everything except love. Love—his only protection, his only weapon, his only method.

*E. Stanley Jones*

He loved us not because we're lovable, but because He is love.

*C. S. Lewis*

Jesus is all compassion. He never betrays us.

*Catherine Marshall*

## Today's Prayer

*Dear Jesus, my life has been changed forever by Your love and sacrifice. Today I will praise You, I will honor You, and I will walk with You. Amen*

# Be Aware of Your Blessings

*Therefore, get your minds ready for action, being self-disciplined, and set your hope completely on the grace to be brought to you at the revelation of Jesus Christ.*

1 Peter 1:13 HCSB

Because we have been so richly blessed, we should make thanksgiving a habit, a regular part of our daily routines. But sometimes, amid the stresses and obligations of everyday life, we may allow interruptions and distractions to interfere with the time we spend with God.

Have you counted your blessings today? And have you thanked God for them? Hopefully so. After all, God's gifts include your family, your friends, your talents, your opportunities, your possessions, and the priceless gift of eternal life. How glorious are these gifts . . . and God is responsible for every one of them.

So today, as you go about the duties of everyday life, pause and give thanks to the Creator. He deserves your praise, and you deserve the experience of praising Him.

Jesus intended for us to be overwhelmed by the blessings of regular days. He said it was the reason he had come: "I am come that they might have life, and that they might have it more abundantly."

*Gloria Gaither*

Think of the blessings we so easily take for granted: Life itself; preservation from danger; every bit of health we enjoy; every hour of liberty; the ability to see, to hear, to speak, to think, and to imagine all this comes from the hand of God.

*Billy Graham*

There is no secret that can separate you from God's love; there is no secret that can separate you from His blessings; there is no secret that is worth keeping from His grace.

*Serita Ann Jakes*

## Today's Prayer

*Lord, let me count my blessings, and let me be Your faithful servant as I give praise to the Giver of all things good. You have richly blessed my life, Lord. Let me, in turn, be a blessing to all those who cross my path, and may the glory be Yours forever. Amen*

# Choosing to Be Kind

*And may the Lord make you increase and abound in love to one another and to all.*

*1 Thessalonians 3:12 NKJV*

Christ showed His love for us by willingly sacrificing His own life so that we might have eternal life: "But God demonstrates his own love for us in this: While we were still sinners, Christ died for us" (Romans 5:8 NIV). We, as Christ's followers, are challenged to share His love with kind words on our lips and praise in our hearts.

Just as Christ has been—and will always be—the ultimate friend to His flock, so should we be Christlike in the kindness and generosity that we show toward others, especially those who are most in need.

When we walk each day with Jesus—and obey the commandments found in God's Holy Word—we become worthy ambassadors for Christ. When we share the love of Christ, we share a priceless gift with the world. As His servants, we must do no less.

Kindness in this world will do much to help others, not only to come into the light, but also to grow in grace day by day.

*Fanny Crosby*

All kindness and good deeds, we must keep silent. The result will be an inner reservoir of personality power.

*Catherine Marshall*

The attitude of kindness is everyday stuff like a great pair of sneakers. Not frilly. Not fancy. Just plain and comfortable.

*Barbara Johnson*

## Today's Prayer

*Lord, sometimes this world can become a place of busyness, frustration, and confusion. Slow me down, Lord, that I might see the needs of those around me. Today, help me show mercy to those in need. Today, let me spread kind words of thanksgiving and celebration in honor of Your Son. Today, let forgiveness rule my heart. And every day, Lord, let my love for Christ be reflected through deeds of kindness for those who need the healing touch of the Master's hand. Amen*

# Serve Him

*The greatest among you will be your servant. Whoever exalts himself will be humbled, and whoever humbles himself will be exalted.*

*Matthew 23:11-12 HCSB*

We live in a world that glorifies power, prestige, fame, and money. But the words of Jesus teach us that the most esteemed men and women in this world are not the self-congratulatory leaders of society but are instead the humblest of servants.

Are you willing to become a humble servant for Christ? Are you willing to pitch in and make the world a better place, or are you determined to keep all your blessings to yourself. The answers to these questions will determine the quality and the direction of your day and your life.

Today, you may feel the temptation to take more than you give. You may be tempted to withhold your generosity. Or you may be tempted to build yourself up in the eyes of your friends. Resist those temptations. Instead, serve your friends quietly and without fanfare. Find a need and fill it . . . humbly. Lend a helping hand . . . anonymously. Share a word of kindness . . . with quiet sincerity. As you go about your daily activities, remember that the Savior of all humanity made Himself a servant, and we, as His followers, must do no less.

---

In the very place where God has put us, whatever its limitations, whatever kind of work it may be, we may indeed serve the Lord Christ.

*Elisabeth Elliot*

God wants us to serve Him with a willing spirit, one that would choose no other way.

*Beth Moore*

Through our service to others, God wants to influence our world for Him.

*Vonette Bright*

## Today's Prayer

*Dear Lord, let me help others in every way that I can. Jesus served others; I can too. I will serve other people with my good deeds and with my prayers. And I will give thanks for everybody who helps me. Amen*

# He Offers Peace

*Peace I leave with you; My peace I give to you; not as the world gives do I give to you. Do not let your heart be troubled, nor let it be fearful.*

John 14:27 NASB

These are turbulent times, difficult days when worries are easy to identify and peace may be a scarce commodity. But no times are too turbulent for God. And if you sincerely desire the peace that passes all understanding, you'll find it in Him.

The familiar words of John 14:27 remind us that Jesus offers us peace, not as the world gives, but as He alone gives. Have you found the genuine peace that can be yours through Jesus Christ? Or are you still rushing after the illusion of "peace and happiness" that the world promises but cannot deliver?

When you welcome God's love into your heart, your life will be transformed as the Father's peace will become yours. And then, because you possess the gift of peace, you can share that gift with family members, with friends, and with coworkers.

This day, complete with its assortment of ups and downs, is a gift from the Creator. This day will contain many blessings. This day will provide quiet moments for prayer and praise. And, this day offers yet another opportunity to welcome the Father into your heart and to share His good news with the world. So honor Him and thank Him: It's the right thing to do—in good times and in hard times—and it's the peaceful way to live.

---

Sometimes we get tired of the burdens of life, but we know that Jesus Christ will meet us at the end of life's journey. And, that makes all the difference.

*Billy Graham*

God cannot give us happiness and peace apart from Himself, because it is not there. There is no such thing.

*C. S. Lewis*

Peace does not mean to be in a place where there is no noise, trouble, or hard work. Peace means to be in the midst of all those things and still be calm in your heart.

*Catherine Marshall*

## Today's Prayer

*Dear Lord, I will open my heart to You. And I thank You, God, for Your love, for Your peace, and for Your Son. Amen*

# Beyond Worry

*Blessed is he that trusts in the Lord.*

*Proverbs 16:20 NIV*

Because we are imperfect human beings, we worry. Even though we are Christians who have been given the assurance of salvation—even though we are Christians who have received the promise of God's love and protection—we find ourselves fretting over the countless details of everyday life. Jesus understood our concerns when He spoke the reassuring words found in Matthew 6: "Therefore I tell you, do not worry about your life . . ."

As you consider the promises of Jesus, remember that God still sits in His heaven and you are His beloved child. Then, perhaps, you will worry a little less and trust God a little more, and that's as it should be because God is trustworthy . . . and you are protected.

I've read the last page of the Bible. It's all going to turn out all right.

*Billy Graham*

We are not called to be burden-bearers, but cross-bearers and light-bearers. We must cast our burdens on the Lord.

*Corrie ten Boom*

It is not work that kills, but worry. And, it is amazing how much wear and tear the human mind and spirit can stand if it is free from friction and well-oiled by the Spirit.

*Vance Havner*

It has been well said that no man ever sank under the burden of the day. It is when tomorrow's burden is added to the burden of today that the weight is more than a man can bear. Never load yourselves so, my friends. If you find yourselves so loaded, at least remember this: it is your own doing, not God's. He begs you to leave the future to Him and mind the present.

*George MacDonald*

## Today's Prayer

*Forgive me, Lord, when I worry. Worry reflects a lack of trust in You. Help me to work, Lord, and not to worry. And, keep me mindful, Father, that nothing, absolutely nothing, will happen this day that You and I cannot handle together. Amen*

# Let Jesus Guide the Way

*I have come as a light into the world, so that everyone who believes in Me would not remain in darkness.*

John 12:46 HCSB

Is Jesus the cornerstone of your life . . . or have you relegated Him to a far corner of your life? The answer to this question will determine the quality, the direction, the tone, and the ultimate destination of your life here on earth and your life throughout eternity.

Thomas Brooks spoke for believers of every generation when he observed, "Christ is the sun, and all the watches of our lives should be set by the dial of his motion." Christ, indeed, is the ultimate Savior of mankind and the personal Savior of those who believe in Him. As His servants, we should place Him at the very center of our lives. And every day that God gives us breath, we should share Christ's love and His message with a world that needs both.

The dearest friend on earth is but a mere shadow compared with Jesus Christ.

*Oswald Chambers*

When we are in a situation where Jesus is all we have, we soon discover he is all we really need.

*Gigi Graham Tchividjian*

In your greatest weakness, turn to your greatest strength, Jesus, and hear Him say, "My grace is sufficient for you, for My strength is made perfect in weakness" (2 Corinthians 12:9, NKJV).

*Lisa Whelchel*

Jesus be mine forever, my God, my heaven, my all.

*C. H. Spurgeon*

## Today's Prayer

*Dear Jesus, You are my Savior and my protector. Give me the courage to trust You completely. Today, I will praise You, I will honor You, and I will live according to Your commandments. Amen*

# Pray for Perspective and Never Lose Hope

*All I'm doing right now, friends, is showing how these things pertain to Apollos and me so that you will learn restraint and not rush into making judgments without knowing all the facts. It is important to look at things from God's point of view. I would rather not see you inflating or deflating reputations based on mere hearsay.*

1 Corinthians 4:6 MSG

If a temporary loss of perspective has left you worried, exhausted, or both, it's time to readjust your thought patterns. Negative thoughts are habit-forming; thankfully, so are positive ones. With practice, you can form the habit of focusing on God's priorities and your own possibilities. When you do, you'll soon discover that you will spend less time fretting about your challenges and more time praising God for His gifts.

When you call upon the Lord and prayerfully seek His will, He will give you wisdom and perspective. When you make God's priorities your priorities, He will direct your steps and calm your fears. So today and every day hereafter, pray for a sense of balance and perspective. And remember: no problems are too big for God—and that includes yours.

Attitude is the mind's paintbrush; it can color any situation.

*Barbara Johnson*

Like a shadow declining swiftly…away…like the dew of the morning gone with the heat of the day; like the wind in the treetops, like a wave of the sea, so are our lives on earth when seen in light of eternity.

*Ruth Bell Graham*

Earthly fears are no fears at all. Answer the big questions of eternity, and the little questions of life fall into perspective.

*Max Lucado*

Instead of being frustrated and overwhelmed by all that is going on in our world, go to the Lord and ask Him to give you His eternal perspective.

*Kay Arthur*

## Today's Prayer

*Dear Lord, give me wisdom and perspective. Guide me according to Your plans for my life and according to Your commandments. And keep me mindful, Dear Lord, that Your truth is—and will forever be—the ultimate truth. Amen*

# When Mountains Need Moving

*I assure you: If anyone says to this mountain, "Be lifted up and thrown into the sea," and does not doubt in his heart, but believes that what he says will happen, it will be done for him.*

*Mark 11:23 HCSB*

When a suffering woman sought healing by simply touching the hem of His garment, Jesus turned and said, "Daughter, be of good comfort; thy faith hath made thee whole" (Matthew 9:22 KJV). We, too, can be made whole when we place our faith completely and unwaveringly in the person of Jesus Christ.

Concentration camp survivor Corrie ten Boom relied on faith during her ten months of imprisonment and torture. Later, despite the fact that four of her family members had died in Nazi death camps, Corrie's faith was unshaken. She wrote, "There is no pit so deep that God's love is not deeper still." Christians take note: Genuine faith in God means faith in all circumstances, happy or sad, joyful or tragic.

If your faith is being tested to the point of breaking, know that your Savior is near. If you reach out to Him in faith, He will give you peace and heal your broken spirit.

Be content to touch even the smallest fragment of the Master's garment, and He will make you whole.

---

Faith is seeing light with the eyes of your heart, when the eyes of your body see only darkness.

*Barbara Johnson*

Just as our faith strengthens our prayer life, so do our prayers deepen our faith. Let us pray often, starting today, for a deeper, more powerful faith.

*Shirley Dobson*

It may be the most difficult time of your life. You may be enduring your own whirlwind. But the whirlwind is a temporary experience. Your faithful, caring Lord will see you through.

*Charles Swindoll*

## Today's Prayer

*Lord, sometimes this world is a terrifying place. When I am filled with uncertainty and doubt, give me faith. In life's dark moments, help me remember that You are always near and that You can overcome any challenge. Today, Lord, and forever, I will place my trust in You. Amen*

# Finding Peace in God's Word

*All Scripture is inspired by God and is profitable for teaching, for rebuking, for correcting, for training in righteousness, so that the man of God may be complete, equipped for every good work.*

*2 Timothy 3:16-17 HCSB*

The words of Matthew 4:4 remind us that, "Man shall not live by bread alone but by every word that proceedeth out of the mouth of God" (KJV). As believers, we must study the Bible and meditate upon its meaning for our lives. Otherwise, we deprive ourselves of a priceless gift from our Creator.

God's Word is unlike any other book. The Bible is a roadmap for life here on earth and for life eternal. As Christians, we are called upon to study God's Holy Word, to follow its commandments, and to share its Good News with the world.

Jonathan Edwards advised, "Be assiduous in reading the Holy Scriptures. This is the fountain whence all knowledge in divinity must be derived. Therefore let not this treasure lie by you neglected." God's Holy Word is, indeed, a priceless, one-of-a-kind treasure, and a passing acquaintance with the Good Book is insufficient for Christians who seek to obey God's Word and to understand His will. After all, man does not live by bread alone . . .

---

The strength that we claim from God's Word does not depend on circumstances. Circumstances will be difficult, but our strength will be sufficient.

*Corrie ten Boom*

God has given us all sorts of counsel and direction in his written Word; thank God, we have it written down in black and white.

*John Eldredge*

Weave the fabric of God's word through your heart and mind. It will hold strong, even if the rest of life unravels.

*Gigi Graham Tchividjian*

## Today's Prayer

*Heavenly Father, Your Word is a light unto the world; I will study it and trust it, and share it. In all that I do, help me be a worthy witness for You as I share the Good News of Your perfect Son and Your perfect Word. Amen*

# The Gift of Cheerfulness

*Worry is a heavy load, but a kind word cheers you up.*

Proverbs 12:25 NCV

Cheerfulness is a gift that we give to others and to ourselves. And, as believers who have been saved by a risen Christ, why shouldn't we be cheerful? The answer, of course, is that we have every reason to honor our Savior with joy in our hearts, smiles on our faces, and words of celebration on our lips.

Christ promises us lives of abundance and joy if we accept His love and His grace. Yet sometimes, even the most righteous among us are beset by fits of ill temper and frustration. During these moments, we may not feel like turning our thoughts and prayers to Christ, but that's precisely what we should do. When we do so, we simply can't stay grumpy for long.

It is not fitting, when one is in God's service, to have a gloomy face or a chilling look.

*St. Francis of Assisi*

One of the great needs in the church today is for every Christian to become enthusiastic about his faith in Jesus Christ.

*Billy Graham*

We act as though comfort and luxury were the chief requirements of life, when all we need to make us really happy is something to be enthusiastic about.

*Charles Kingsley*

We may run, walk, stumble, drive, or fly, but let us never lose sight of the reason for the journey, or miss a chance to see a rainbow on the way.

*Gloria Gaither*

## Today's Prayer

*Your love is a perfect love, O Lord. Let me accept Your love today, and let me share it with my loved ones.  Amen*

# Focusing on God

*Give your entire attention to what God is doing right now, and don't get worked up about what may or may not happen tomorrow. God will help you deal with whatever hard things come up when the time comes.*

Matthew 6:34 MSG

All of us may find our courage tested by the inevitable disappointments and tragedies of life. After all, ours is a world filled with uncertainty, hardship, sickness, and danger. Trouble, it seems, is never too far from the front door.

When we focus upon our fears and our doubts, we may find many reasons to lie awake at night and fret about the uncertainties of the coming day. A better strategy, of course, is to focus not upon our fears, but instead upon our God.

God is as near as your next breath, and He is in control. He offers salvation to all His children, including you. God is your shield and your strength; you are His forever. So don't focus your thoughts upon the fears of the day. Instead, trust God's plan and His eternal love for you. And remember: God is good, and He has the last word.

His hand on me is a father's hand, gently guiding and encouraging. His hand lets me know he is with me, so I am not afraid.

*Mary Morrison Suggs*

Ignoring Him by neglecting prayer and Bible reading will cause you to doubt.

*Anne Graham Lotz*

Whether our fear is absolutely realistic or out of proportion in our minds, our greatest refuge is Jesus Christ.

*Luci Swindoll*

Fear and doubt are conquered by a faith that rejoices. And faith can rejoice because the promises of God are as certain as God Himself.

*Kay Arthur*

## Today's Prayer

*Your Word reminds me, Lord, that even when I walk through the valley of the shadow of death, I need fear no evil, for You are with me, and You comfort me. Thank You, Lord, for a perfect love that casts out fear. Let me live courageously and faithfully this day and every day. Amen*

# The Decision to Celebrate Life

*This is the day the Lord has made; let us rejoice and be glad in it.*

Psalm 118:24 HCSB

God gives us this day; He fills it to the brim with possibilities, and He challenges us to use it for His purposes. The 118th Psalm reminds us that today, like every other day, is a cause for celebration. The day is presented to us fresh and clean at midnight, free of charge, but we must beware: Today is a non-renewable resource—once it's gone, it's gone forever. Our responsibility, of course, is to use this day in the service of God's will and according to His commandments.

Today, treasure the time that God has given you. Give Him the glory and the praise and the thanksgiving that He deserves. And search for the hidden possibilities that God has placed along your path. This day is a priceless gift from God, so use it joyfully and encourage others to do likewise. After all, this is the day the Lord has made.

According to Jesus, it is God's will that His children be filled with the joy of life.

*Catherine Marshall*

If you can forgive the person you were, accept the person you are, and believe in the person you will become, you are headed for joy. So celebrate your life.

*Barbara Johnson*

Christ is the secret, the source, the substance, the center, and the circumference of all true and lasting gladness.

*Mrs. Charles E. Cowman*

When the dream of our heart is one that God has planted there, a strange happiness flows into us. At that moment, all of the spiritual resources of the universe are released to help us. Our praying is then at one with the will of God and becomes a channel for the Creator's purposes for us and our world.

*Catherine Marshall*

## Today's Prayer

*Dear Lord, help me remember that every day is cause for celebration. Today I will try my best to keep joy in my heart. I will celebrate the life You have given me here on earth and the eternal life that will be mine in heaven. Amen*

# Be Optimistic

*My cup runs over. Surely goodness and mercy shall follow me all the days of my life; and I will dwell in the house of the Lord Forever.*

*Psalm 23:5-6 NKJV*

Are you an optimistic, hopeful, enthusiastic Christian? You should be. After all, as a believer, you have every reason to be optimistic about life here on earth and life eternal. As C. H. Spurgeon observed, "Our hope in Christ for the future is the mainstream of our joy." But sometimes, you may find yourself pulled down by the inevitable demands and worries of life here on earth. If you find yourself discouraged, stressed, or both, then it's time to take your concerns to God. When you do, He will lift your spirits and renew your strength.

Today, make this promise to yourself and keep it: vow to be a hope-filled Christian. Think optimistically about your life, your profession, your family, and your future. Trust your hopes, not your fears. Take time to celebrate God's glorious creation. And then, when you've filled your heart with hope and gladness, share your optimism with others. They'll be better for it, and so will you.

The popular idea of faith is of a certain obstinate optimism: the hope, tenaciously held in the face of trouble, that the universe is fundamentally friendly and things may get better.

*J. I. Packer*

The people whom I have seen succeed best in life have always been cheerful and hopeful people who went about their business with a smile on their faces.

*Charles Kingsley*

Go forward confidently, energetically attacking problems, expecting favorable outcomes.

*Norman Vincent Peale*

No Christian can be a pessimist, for Christianity is a system of radical optimism.

*William Ralph Inge*

## Today's Prayer

*Dear Lord, I will look for the best in other people, I will expect the best from You, and I will try my best to do my best—today and every day. Amen*

# Let God Decide

*A man's heart plans his way, but the Lord directs his steps.*

*Proverbs 16:9 NKJV*

The world will often lead you astray, but God will not. His counsel leads you to Himself, which, of course, is the path He has always intended for you to take. Are you facing a difficult decision, a troubling circumstance, or a powerful temptation? If so, it's time to step back, to stop focusing on the world, and to focus, instead, on the will of your Father in heaven.

Everyday living is an exercise in decision-making. Today and every day you must make choices: choices about what you will do, what you will worship, and how you will think. When in doubt, make choices that you sincerely believe will bring you to a closer relationship with God. And if you're uncertain of your next step, pray about it. When you do, answers will come—the right answers for you.

God always gives His best to those who leave the choice with Him.

*Jim Elliot*

There is no need to fear the decisions of life when you know Jesus Christ, for His name is Counselor.

*Warren Wiersbe*

The Reference Point for the Christian is the Bible. All values, judgments, and attitudes must be gauged in relationship to this Reference Point.

*Ruth Bell Graham*

I don't doubt that the Holy Spirit guides your decisions from within when you make them with the intention of pleasing God. The error would be to think that He speaks only within, whereas in reality He speaks also through Scripture, the Church, Christian friends, and books.

*C. S. Lewis*

## Today's Prayer

*Lord, help me to make decisions that are pleasing to You. Help me to be honest, patient, thoughtful, and obedient. And above all, help me to follow the teachings of Jesus, not just today, but every day. Amen*

# Be Patient, Be Hopeful, and Trust God

*Trust in Him at all times, you people; pour out your heart before Him; God is a refuge for us.*

*Psalm 62:8 NKJV*

Psalm 37:7 commands us to wait patiently for God. But as busy people in a fast-paced world, many of us find that waiting quietly for God is difficult. Why? Because we are fallible human beings seeking to live according to our own timetables, not God's. In our better moments, we realize that patience is not only a virtue, but it is also a commandment from God.

We human beings are impatient by nature. We know what we want, and we know exactly when we want it: NOW! But, God knows better. He has created a world that unfolds according to His plans, not our own. As believers, we must trust His wisdom and His goodness.

God instructs us to be patient in all things. We must be patient with our families, our friends, and our associates. We must also be patient with our Creator as He unfolds His plan for our lives. And that's as it should be. After all, think how patient God has been with us.

God never hurries. There are no deadlines against which He must work. To know this is to quiet our spirits and relax our nerves.

*A. W. Tozer*

Waiting is the hardest kind of work, but God knows best, and we may joyfully leave all in His hands.

*Lottie Moon*

As we wait on God, He helps us use the winds of adversity to soar above our problems. As the Bible says, "Those who wait on the LORD . . . shall mount up with wings like eagles."

*Billy Graham*

How do you wait upon the Lord? First you must learn to sit at His feet and take time to listen to His words.

*Kay Arthur*

## Today's Prayer

*Lord, give me patience. When I am hurried, give me peace. When I am frustrated, give me perspective. When I am angry, let me turn my heart to You. Today, let me become a more patient person, Dear Lord, as I trust in You and in Your master plan for my life. Amen*

# The Shepherd's Gift

*My cup runs over. Surely goodness and mercy shall follow me all the days of my life; and I will dwell in the house of the Lord forever.*

*Psalm 23:5-6 NKJV*

When we entrust our hearts and our days to the One who created us, we experience abundance through the grace and sacrifice of His Son. But, when we turn our thoughts and direct our energies away from God's commandments, we inevitably forfeit the spiritual abundance that might otherwise be ours.

Do you sincerely seek the riches that our Savior offers to those who give themselves to Him? Then follow Him completely and obey Him without reservation. When you do, you will receive the love and the abundance that He has promised. Seek first the salvation that is available through a personal relationship with Jesus Christ, and then claim the joy, the peace, and the spiritual abundance that the Shepherd offers His sheep.

God is the giver, and we are the receivers. And His richest gifts are bestowed not upon those who do the greatest things, but upon those who accept His abundance and His grace.

*Hannah Whitall Smith*

Instead of living a black-and-white existence, we'll be released into a Technicolor world of vibrancy and emotion when we more accurately reflect His nature to the world around us.

*Bill Hybels*

God's riches are beyond anything we could ask or even dare to imagine! If my life gets gooey and stale, I have no excuse.

*Barbara Johnson*

Jesus wants Life for us, Life with a capital L.

*John Eldredge*

## Today's Prayer

*Good Shepherd, thank You for the abundant life that is mine through Christ Jesus. Guide me according to Your will, and help me to be a worthy servant in all that I say and do. Give me courage, Lord, to claim the rewards You have promised, and when I do, let the glory be Yours. Amen*

# Trust Him When Times Are Tough

*Blessed be the God and Father of our Lord Jesus Christ, the Father of mercies and the God of all comfort. He comforts us in all our affliction, so that we may be able to comfort those who are in any kind of affliction, through the comfort we ourselves receive from God.*

*2 Corinthians 1:3-4 HCSB*

The Bible promises this: tough times are temporary but God's love is not—God's love lasts forever. So what does that mean to you? Just this: From time to time, everybody faces tough times, and so will you. And when tough times arrive, God will always stand ready to protect you and heal you.

Psalm 147 promises, "He heals the brokenhearted" (v. 3, NIV), but Psalm 147 doesn't say that He heals them instantly. Usually, it takes time (and maybe even a little help from you) for God to fix things. So if you're facing tough times, face them with God by your side. If you find yourself in any kind of trouble, pray about it and ask God for help. And be patient. God will work things out, just as He has promised, but He will do it in His own way and in His own time.

Measure the size of the obstacles against the size of God.

*Beth Moore*

If we're going to stand up and make a difference for Christ while others lounge about, you can be sure we'll encounter hardships, obstacles, nuisances, hassles, and inconveniences—much more than the average couch potato. And we shouldn't be surprised. Such difficulty while serving Christ isn't necessarily suffering—it's status quo.

*Joni Eareckson Tada*

The only way to learn a strong faith is to endure great trials. I have learned my faith by standing firm amid the most severe of tests.

*George Mueller*

## Today's Prayer

*Dear Heavenly Father, You are my strength and my protector. When I am troubled, You comfort me. When I am discouraged, You lift me up. When I am afraid, You deliver me. Let me turn to You, Lord, when I am weak. In times of adversity, let me trust Your plan and Your will for my life. Your love is infinite, as is Your wisdom. Whatever my circumstances, Dear Lord, let me always give the praise, and the thanks, and the glory to You. Amen*

# Perspective for Today

*Don't turn your back on wisdom, for she will protect you.*
*Love her, and she will guard you.*

*Proverbs 4:6 NLT*

Sometimes, amid the demands of daily life, we lose perspective. Life seems out of balance, and the pressures of everyday living seem overwhelming. What's needed is a fresh perspective, a restored sense of balance…and God.

If a temporary loss of perspective has left you worried, exhausted, or both, it's time to readjust your thought patterns. Negative thoughts are habit-forming; thankfully, so are positive ones. With practice, you can form the habit of focusing on God's priorities and your possibilities. When you do, you'll soon discover that you will spend less time fretting about your challenges and more time praising God for His gifts.

When you call upon the Lord and prayerfully seek His will, He will give you wisdom and perspective. When you make God's priorities your priorities, He will direct your steps and calm your fears. So today and every day hereafter, pray for a sense of balance and perspective. And remember: your thoughts are intensely powerful things, so handle them with care.

Instead of being frustrated and overwhelmed by all that is going on in our world, go to the Lord and ask Him to give you His eternal perspective.

*Kay Arthur*

Like a shadow declining swiftly…away…like the dew of the morning gone with the heat of the day; like the wind in the treetops, like a wave of the sea, so are our lives on earth when seen in light of eternity.

*Ruth Bell Graham*

Earthly fears are no fears at all. Answer the big questions of eternity, and the little questions of life fall into perspective.

*Max Lucado*

The proper perspective creates within us a spirit of reaching outside of ourselves with joy and enthusiasm.

*Luci Swindoll*

## Today's Prayer

*Dear Lord, when the pace of my life becomes frantic, slow me down and give me perspective. Give me the wisdom to realize that the problems of today are only temporary but that Your love is eternal. When I become discouraged, keep me steady and sure, so that I might do Your will here on earth and then live with You forever in heaven. Amen*

# Pleasing God

*But neither exile nor homecoming is the main thing. Cheerfully pleasing God is the main thing, and that's what we aim to do, regardless of our conditions.*

2 Corinthians 5:9 MSG

When God made you, He equipped you with an array of talents and abilities that are uniquely yours. It's up to you to discover those talents and to use them, but sometimes the world will encourage you to do otherwise. At times, society will attempt to cubbyhole you, to standardize you, and to make you fit into a particular, preformed mold. Sometimes, because you're an imperfect human being, you may become so wrapped up in meeting society's expectations that you fail to focus on God's expectations. To do so is a mistake of major proportions—don't make it.

Who will you try to please today: God or man? Your primary obligation is not to please imperfect men and women. Your obligation is to strive diligently to meet the expectations of an all-knowing and perfect God. Trust Him always. Love Him always. Praise Him always. And seek to please Him. Always.

It is impossible to please God doing things motivated by and produced by the flesh.

*Bill Bright*

Whether we think of, or speak to, God, whether we act or suffer for him, all is prayer when we have no other object than his love and the desire of pleasing him.

*John Wesley*

God is not hard to please. He does not expect us to be absolutely perfect. He just expects us to keep moving toward Him and believing in Him, letting Him work with us to bring us into conformity to His will and ways.

*Joyce Meyer*

All our offerings, whether music or martyrdom, are like the intrinsically worthless present of a child, which a father values indeed, but values only for the intention.

*C. S. Lewis*

## Today's Prayer

*Dear Lord, today I will honor You with my thoughts, my actions, and my prayers. I will seek to please You, and I will strive to serve You. Your blessings are as limitless as Your love. And because I have been so richly blessed, I will worship You, Father, with thanksgiving in my heart and praise on my lips, this day and forever. Amen*

# Have the Courage to Trust God

*Trust in the Lord with all your heart, and do not rely on your own understanding; think about Him in all your ways, and He will guide you on the right paths.*

Proverbs 3:5-6 HCSB

Sometimes the future seems bright, and sometimes it does not. Yet even when we cannot see the possibilities of tomorrow, God can. As believers, our challenge is to trust an uncertain future to an all-powerful God.

When we trust God, we should trust Him without reservation. We should steel ourselves against the inevitable stresses of the day, secure in the knowledge that our Heavenly Father has a plan for the future that only He can see.

Can you place your future into the hands of a loving and all-knowing God? Can you live amid the uncertainties of today, knowing that God has dominion over all your tomorrows? If you can, you are wise and you are blessed. When you trust God with everything you are and everything you have, He will bless you now and forever.

Do not be afraid, then, that if you trust, or tell others to trust, the matter will end there. Trust is only the beginning and the continual foundation. When we trust Him, the Lord works, and His work is the important part of the whole matter.

*Hannah Whitall Smith*

Sometimes the very essence of faith is trusting God in the midst of things He knows good and well we cannot comprehend.

*Beth Moore*

Are you serious about wanting God's guidance to become the person he wants you to be? The first step is to tell God that you know you can't manage your own life; that you need his help.

*Catherine Marshall*

## Today's Prayer

*Dear Lord, let my faith be in You, and in You alone. Without You, I am weak, but when I trust You, I am protected. In every aspect of my life, Father, let me place my hope and my trust in Your infinite wisdom and Your boundless grace. Amen*

# Perseverance and Hope

*But thanks be to God, who gives us the victory through our Lord Jesus Christ. Therefore, my beloved brethren, be steadfast, immovable, always abounding in the work of the Lord, knowing that your labor is not in vain in the Lord.*

*1 Corinthians 15:57-58 NKJV*

A well-lived life is like a marathon, not a sprint—it calls for preparation, determination, and, of course, lots of perseverance. As an example of perfect perseverance, we Christians need look no further than our Savior, Jesus Christ.

Jesus finished what He began. Despite His suffering and despite the shame of the cross, Jesus was steadfast in His faithfulness to God. We, too, must remain faithful, especially during times of hardship. Sometimes, God may answer our prayers with silence, and when He does, we must patiently persevere.

Are you facing a tough situation? If so, remember this: whatever your problem, God can handle it. Your job is to keep persevering until He does.

We don't give up. We look up. We trust. We believe. And our optimism is not hollow. Christ has proven worthy. He has shown that he never fails. That's what makes God, God.

*Max Lucado*

Stand still and refuse to retreat. Look at it as God looks at it and draw upon his power to hold up under the blast.

*Charles Swindoll*

Just remember, every flower that ever bloomed had to go through a whole lot of dirt to get there!

*Barbara Johnson*

Failure is one of life's most powerful teachers. How we handle our failures determines whether we're going to simply "get by" in life or "press on."

*Beth Moore*

## Today's Prayer

*Lord, when life is difficult, I am tempted to abandon hope in the future. But You are my God, and I can draw strength from You. Let me trust You, Father, in good times and in bad times. Let me persevere—even if my soul is troubled—and let me follow Your Son, Jesus Christ, this day and forever. Amen*

# Pray About Your Decisions

*Now if any of you lacks wisdom, he should ask God, who gives to all generously and without criticizing, and it will be given to him. But let him ask in faith without doubting. For the doubter is like the surging sea, driven and tossed by the wind.*

*James 1:5-6 HCSB*

Have you fervently asked God for His guidance in every aspect of your life? If so, then you're continually inviting your Creator to reveal Himself in a variety of ways. As a follower of Christ, you must do no less.

Jesus made it clear to His disciples: they should pray always. So should we. Genuine, heartfelt prayer produces powerful changes in us and in our world. When we lift our hearts to our Father in heaven, we open ourselves to a never-ending source of divine wisdom and infinite love.

Do you have questions about your future that you simply can't answer? Ask for the guidance of your Heavenly Father. Do you sincerely seek to know God's purpose for your life? Then ask Him for direction—and keep asking Him every day that you live. Whatever your need, no matter how great or small, pray about it and never lose hope.

Are you weak? Weary? Confused? Troubled? Pressured? How is your relationship with God? Is it held in its place of priority? I believe the greater the pressure, the greater your need for time alone with Him.

*Kay Arthur*

When there is a matter that requires definite prayer, pray until you believe God and until you can thank Him for His answer.

*Hannah Whitall Smith*

A prayerful heart and an obedient heart will learn, very slowly and not without sorrow, to stake everything on God Himself.

*Elisabeth Elliot*

Prayer is the same as the breathing of air for the lungs. Exhaling makes us get rid of our dirty air. Inhaling gives clean air. To exhale is to confess, to inhale is to be filled with the Holy Spirit.

*Corrie ten Boom*

## Today's Prayer

*Dear Lord, today, I will pray about matters great and small. I will bring my concerns to You, Father. I will listen for Your voice, and I will follow in the footsteps of Your Son. Amen*

# Live on Purpose

*I, therefore, the prisoner in the Lord, urge you to walk worthy of the calling you have received.*

*Ephesians 4:1 HCSB*

"What on earth does God intend for me to do with my life?" It's an easy question to ask but, for many of us, a difficult question to answer. Why? Because God's purposes aren't always clear to us. Sometimes we wander aimlessly in a wilderness of our own making. And sometimes, we struggle mightily against God in an unsuccessful attempt to find success and happiness through our own means, not His.

If you sincerely seek God's guidance, He will give it. But, He will make His revelations known to you in a way and in a time of His choosing, not yours, so be patient. If you prayerfully petition God and work diligently to discern His intentions, He will, in time, lead you to a place of joyful abundance and eternal peace.

Sometimes, God's intentions will be clear to you; other times, God's plan will seem uncertain at best. But even on those difficult days when you are unsure which way to turn, you must never lose sight of these overriding facts: God created you for a reason; He has important work for you to do; and He's waiting patiently for you to do it.

Whatever clouds you face today, ask Jesus, the light of the world, to help you look behind the cloud to see His glory and His plans for you.

*Billy Graham*

Yesterday is just experience but tomorrow is glistening with purpose—and today is the channel leading from one to the other.

*Barbara Johnson*

Only God's chosen task for you will ultimately satisfy. Do not wait until it is too late to realize the privilege of serving Him in His chosen position for you.

*Beth Moore*

In the very place where God has put us, whatever its limitations, whatever kind of work it may be, we may indeed serve the Lord Christ.

*Elisabeth Elliot*

## Today's Prayer

*Dear Lord, I know that You have a purpose for my life, and I will seek that purpose today and every day that I live. Let my actions be pleasing to You, and let me share Your Good News with a world that so desperately needs Your healing hand and the salvation of Your Son. Amen*

# In Difficult Times, God Teaches and Leads

*Leave inexperience behind, and you will live; pursue the way of understanding.*

*Proverbs 9:6 HCSB*

Complete spiritual maturity is never achieved in a day, or in a year, or even in a lifetime. The journey toward spiritual maturity is an ongoing process that continues, day by day, throughout every stage of life. Every stage of life has its opportunities and its challenges, and if we're wise, we continue to seek God's guidance as each new chapter of life unfolds.

From time to time, all of us encounter circumstances that test our faith. When we encounter life's inevitable tragedies, trials, uncertainties, and disappointments, we may be tempted to blame God or to rebel against Him. But the Bible reminds us that the trials of life should be viewed as opportunities for growth: "Consider it a great joy, my brothers, whenever you experience various trials, knowing that the testing of your faith produces endurance. But endurance must do its complete work, so that you may be mature and complete, lacking nothing" (James 1:2-4 HCSB).

Have you recently encountered one of life's inevitable tests? If so, remember that God still has lessons that He intends to teach you. So ask yourself this: what lesson is God trying to teach me today?

---

Your greatest ministry will likely come out of your greatest hurt.

*Rick Warren*

You were born with tremendous potential. When you were born again through faith in Jesus Christ, God added spiritual gifts to your natural talents.

*Warren Wiersbe*

## Today's Prayer

*Dear Lord, when I open myself to You, I am blessed. Let me accept Your love and Your wisdom, Father. Show me Your way, and deliver me from the painful mistakes that I make when I stray from Your commandments. Let me live according to Your Word, and let me grow in my faith every day that I live. Amen*

# Commissioned to Witness

*Therefore go and make disciples of all nations, baptizing them in the name of the Father and of the Son and of the Holy Spirit, and teaching them to obey everything I have commanded you. And surely I am with you always, to the very end of the age.*

*Matthew 28:19-20 NIV*

After His resurrection, Jesus addressed His disciples. As recorded in the 28th chapter of Matthew, Christ instructed His followers to share His message with the world. This "Great Commission" applies to Christians of every generation, including our own.

As believers, we are called to share the Good News of Jesus with our families, with our neighbors, and with the world. Christ commanded His disciples to become fishers of men. We must do likewise, and we must do so today. Tomorrow may indeed be too late.

To stand in an uncaring world and say, "See, here is the Christ" is a daring act of courage.

*Calvin Miller*

Our commission is quite specific. We are told to be His witness to all nations. For us, as His disciples, to refuse any part of this commission frustrates the love of Jesus Christ, the Son of God.

*Catherine Marshall*

Witnessing is not something that we do for the Lord; it is something that He does through us if we are filled with the Holy Spirit.

*Warren Wiersbe*

In their heart of hearts, I think all true followers of Christ long to become contagious Christians. Though unsure about how to do so or the risks involved, deep down they sense that there isn't anything as rewarding as opening a person up to God's love and truth.

*Bill Hybels*

## Today's Prayer

*Heavenly Father, every man and woman, every boy and girl is Your child. You desire that all Your children know Jesus as their Lord and Savior. Father, let me be part of Your Great Commission. Let me give, let me pray, and let me go out into this world so that I might be a fisher of men . . . for You. Amen*

# Life Eternal

*Because I live, you will live also.*

*John 14:19 NASB*

Ours is not a distant God. Ours is a God who understands—far better than we ever could—the essence of what it means to be human. How marvelous it is that God became a man and walked among us. Had He not chosen to do so, we might feel removed from a distant Creator.

God understands our hopes, our fears, and our temptations. He understands what it means to be angry and what it costs to forgive. He knows the heart, the conscience, and the soul of every person who has ever lived, including you. And God has a plan of salvation that is intended for you. Accept it. Accept God's gift through the person of His Son Christ Jesus, and then rest assured: God walked among us so that you might have eternal life; amazing though it may seem, He did it for you.

The gift of God is eternal life, spiritual life, abundant life through faith in Jesus Christ, the Living Word of God.

*Anne Graham Lotz*

God loves you and wants you to experience peace and life—abundant and eternal.

*Billy Graham*

Teach us to set our hopes on heaven, to hold firmly to the promise of eternal life, so that we can withstand the struggles and storms of this world.

*Max Lucado*

How completely satisfying to turn from our limitations to a God who has none. Eternal years lie in his heart. For him time does not pass, it remains; and those who are in Christ share with him all the riches of limitless time and endless years.

*A. W. Tozer*

## Today's Prayer

*I know, Lord, that this world is not my home; I am only here for a brief while. And, You have given me the priceless gift of eternal life through Your Son Jesus. Keep the hope of heaven fresh in my heart, and, while I am in this world, help me to pass through it with faith in my heart and praise on my lips . . . for You. Amen*

*A word spoken at the right time*
*is like golden apples on a silver tray.*

—

*Proverbs 25:11 HCSB*